THE CASE FOR LIBERALISM IN AN AGE OF EXTREMISM

OR, WHY I LEFT THE LEFT BUT CAN'T JOIN THE RIGHT

Also by Alan Dershowitz

Defending the Constitution: Alan Dershowitz's Senate Argument Against Impeachment
Guilt by Accusation: The Challenge of Proving Innocence in the Age of #MeToo
Defending Israel: The Story of My Relationship with My Most Challenging Client
The Mueller Report (with an Introduction by Alan Dershowitz)
The Case Against Impeaching Trump
The Case Against BDS: Why Singling Out Israel for Boycott Is Anti-Semitic and Anti-Peace
Trumped Up: How Criminalization of Political Differences Endangers Democracy
Electile Dysfunction: A Guide for Unaroused Voters
The Case Against the Iran Deal
Terror Tunnels: The Case for Israel's Just War Against Hamas
Abraham: The World's First (But Certainly Not Last) Jewish Lawyer
Taking the Stand: My Life in the Law
The Trials of Zion
The Case for Moral Clarity: Israel, Hamas and Gaza
The Case Against Israel's Enemies: Exposing Jimmy Carter and Others Who Stand in the Way of Peace
Is There a Right to Remain Silent? Coercive Interrogation and the Fifth Amendment After 9/11
Finding Jefferson: A Lost Letter, a Remarkable Discovery and the First Amendment in the Age of Terrorism
Blasphemy: How the Religious Right is Hijacking Our Declaration of Independence
Pre-emption: A Knife That Cuts Both Ways
What Israel Meant to Me: By 80 Prominent Writers, Performers, Scholars, Politicians and Journalists
Rights From Wrongs: A Secular Theory of the Origins of Rights
America on Trial: Inside the Legal Battles That Transformed Our Nation
The Case for Peace: How the Arab-Israeli Conflict Can Be Resolved
The Case for Israel
America Declares Independence
Why Terrorism Works: Understanding the Threat, Responding to the Challenge
Shouting Fire: Civil Liberties in a Turbulent Age
Letters to a Young Lawyer
Supreme Injustice: How the High Court Hijacked Election 2000
Genesis of Justice: Ten Stories of Biblical Injustice that Led to the Ten Commandments and Modern Law
Just Revenge
Sexual McCarthyism: Clinton, Starr, and the Emerging Constitutional Crisis
The Vanishing American Jew: In Search of Jewish Identity for the Next Century
Reasonable Doubts: The Criminal Justice System and the O.J. Simpson Case
The Abuse Excuse: And Other Cop-Outs, Stories and Evasions of Responsibility
The Advocate's Devil
Contrary to Popular Opinion
Chutzpah
Taking Liberties: A Decade of Hard Cases, Bad Laws, and Bum Raps
Reversal of Fortune: Inside the Von Bülow Case
The Best Defense
Criminal Law: Theory and Process (with Joseph Goldstein and Richard Schwartz)
Psychoanalysis, Psychiatry, and Law (with Joseph Goldstein and Jay Katz)

THE CASE FOR LIBERALISM IN AN AGE OF EXTREMISM

OR, WHY I LEFT THE LEFT BUT CAN'T JOIN THE RIGHT

ALAN DERSHOWITZ

HOT BOOKS

This book is lovingly dedicated to Ella, Dave, Lori, and Lyle—the generation that we hope will repair our broken world.

Acknowledgments

With a debt of gratitude to my friends and relatives who read the manuscript and offered suggestions, especially Carolyn Cohen, Elon Dershowitz, Ella Dershowitz, David Stern, Stephen Trachtenberg, Bernard Beck, George Lefcoe, Leon Chiu.

My appreciation to Tonya Lederman and Maura Kelley for their work on the manuscript and footnotes, and to my editor, Oren Eades, the cover designer, Brian Peterson, and the publisher, Tony Lyons, for their professionalism and dedication.

Hot Books may be purchased in bulk at special discounts for sales promotion, corporate gifts, fund-raising, or educational purposes. Special editions can also be created to specifications. For details, contact the Special Sales Department, Skyhorse Publishing, 307 West 36th Street, 11th Floor, New York, NY 10018 or info@skyhorsepublishing.com.

Hot Books® and Skyhorse Publishing® are registered trademarks of Skyhorse Publishing, Inc.®, a Delaware corporation.

Visit our website at www.hotbookspress.com.

10 9 8 7 6 5 4 3 2 1

Library of Congress Cataloging-in-Publication Data is available on file.

ISBN: 978-1-5107-6298-5
eBook: 978-1-5107-6299-2

Cover design by Brian Peterson

Printed in the United States of America

Table of Contents

INTRODUCTION

We are living in the most divisive era of modern American history. Our deep and dangerous divisions are moving us in the direction of the kind of malignant extremism that has plagued other countries throughout history. The left is moving further and harder left, and away from traditional liberalism. The right is moving further and harder right, and away from traditional conservatism. The center, which has long been the hallmark of the American character and the key to our success as a nation, is shrinking, and with it, our commitment to reasoned dialogue, principled compromises, tolerance of divergent views, due process of law, freedom of expression and basic fairness. We are witnessing if not the demise, then certainly the weakening, of both centrist liberalism and centrist conservatism, which have both served our nation well throughout our history.

Since I am a liberal, I will make the case in this short book for classic, centrist liberalism. I will leave it to conservatives to make the case for classic, centrist conservatism, though—as I shall show—these philosophies are, at their core, more similar than different in many respects.

Let me be clear that I will not be making the case for the *status quo*, or for a return to some imaginary utopic past. For me, liberalism is a dynamic, adaptive, ever-changing process for improving the world. It must be open to positive new ideas, even some (but certainly not all) of those espoused by radicals. As a conservative critic of liberalism put it: "Liberalism is a restless philosophy. It must always be doing something. To rest, or to express satisfaction with the state of things, is to become conservative."[1]

It is this "restless," dissatisfied, dynamic liberalism that I have lived and loved over my lifetime, and it is that liberalism I advocate in this book and will continue to advocate in the court of public opinion.

My own credentials as a liberal have recently been questioned, despite my life-long devotion to the cause of liberalism.[2] It was as a liberal and civil libertarian that I opposed President Trump's impeachment, despite his illiberalism. That's what liberals do—defend principles, not parties or persons. The attack on my liberalism does not represent a change in my philosophy, which is still what it has always been. It represents a partisan abandonment of true liberalism on the part of some who attack me, and a symptom of the divisiveness we are now experiencing.

I grew up during what I believed were very divisive times. In college, I experienced the aftermath of McCarthyism. I attended law school during the Vietnam War, provided legal assistance to those who refused to be drafted, participated in the civil rights movement, helped defend Senator Ted Kennedy after Chappaquiddick,[3] supported the impeachment of Richard Nixon, represented O.J. Simpson in his racially fraught trial, testified against the impeachment of Bill Clinton, worked for Al Gore during the contested 2000 election, opposed the

---

1 Barton Swaim, "Joe Biden and the Slow Death of Liberalism," *The Wall Street Journal*, April 10, 2020. I'm reminded of the scene from *The Merchant of Venice* where Shylock is asked whether his conversion to Christianity is genuine, and he responds that he is, "content." I have always thought that his answer was revealing, because no Jew is ever content!

2 See, e.g., Darragh Roche, "Alan Dershowitz: Republicans Won't Cancel 2020 Election Because it Would Risk Making Bernie Sanders President," *Politicus*, April 16, 2020. Describing me as a "Conservative Legal Scholar;" Joe Patrice, "Unsatisfied with Just Becoming a Republican, Alan Dershowitz is Going Back in Time to be a Republican All Along." Above the Law, March 11 2020; Grace Tatter, "Week Ahead: There's Impeachment, and Then There's Everything Else." WBUR, Jan 20,2020.

3 When Senator Edward Kennedy drove off the bridge at Chappaquiddick, resulting in the death of Mary Jo Kopechne, I was part of the legal team that represented him and made a deal that was widely criticized as too favorable.

invasion of Iraq, took controversial positions on torture warrants and targeted killings in the aftermath of the 9/11 terrorist attack, represented Jeffrey Epstein, and other despised defendants, and have been vocal in defense of Israel. It is fair to say that I have never shied away from controversy and have lived a highly and controversial public life, with a confrontational approach. As the *Boston Globe* put it: "If Dershowitz is not in your face about something, it's as if he's not doing his job."

But nothing in my past compares in intensity, duration, and impact with the corrosive divisiveness we are experiencing during the Trump administration, even after the partisan House impeachment and Senate acquittal of our 45th President, in which I participated.[4] The Trump presidency, and the reactions to it, have divided families, severed life-long friendships, re-aligned party affiliations, changed our political language, substituted name calling for rational civil discourse, turned networks away from objective reporting into partisan pandering, frightened people into silence, ended tolerance for differing ideas and perspectives, turned classrooms into political platforms, severely compromised civil liberties, and rendered obsolete the classic American symbol "Out of many one." Tragically, we are no longer "one."

Even the Coronavirus pandemic—which should have united all Americans, as other national and international crises did—divided us along partisan lines, with each side blasting the other for not doing enough or for doing too much. The right names it the "Chinese Virus," while the left calls it the "Trump Virus." Conspiracy theories abound on both extremes. The hard-right, led by Alex Jones and his "Infowars" website, exploit the pandemic to incite marchers to demand "the freedom to be infected" and to blame billionaire tech leaders for seeking "population control." Some of the far-left are targeting Israel and the Mossad for spreading the virus.[5] Hard-left anti-vaxxers join hard-right anti-vaxxers in promoting conspiracy theories about the evils of vaccinations and other medically proved preventives or treatments.

---

4 Alan Dershowitz. *Defending the Constitution: Alan Dershowitz's Senate Argument Against Impeachment* (New York: Skyhorse Publishing, 2020).

5 See, e.g., Tom Harris, "The Left Loves Conspiracy Theories Just as Much as the Right," *The Telegraph*, 18 April 2020.

Social science research suggests that "fear of infection increases prejudice and distrust," and that economic crises of the past—such as those in Germany in the early 30s and Greece more recently—led to "increased support for both Communist and National Socialist parties." Professor Paul Conway, who conducted research on these issues, predicted that "for the next decade or so in America and around the world, there will be more intense partisan division…"[6]

The new divisiveness has forced people to take sides and become uncompromising—even on nuanced issues, complex people, and difficult decisions. Seeing virtue in anything the opposing side says or does has become treasonous—giving aid and comfort to the "enemy." As Pogo once put it: "We have met the enemy and he is us!"

During the earlier controversies in my career, some of my ideas and actions were harshly criticized. I was student council president at Brooklyn College when professors who had been subpoenaed to testify about their alleged past associations with the Communist Party, and who had invoked their constitutional right not to incriminate themselves, were labeled, "Fifth Amendment Communists" and fired. Despite my hatred for communism, I stood up for their right to teach and our right to learn from them. The case of *Slochower v. Board of Higher Education*, was decided by the Supreme Court in 1956, when I was a student. Other cases continued in lower courts and agencies for several years. Speakers who were labelled as Communists were banned from the campus.

When I participated in a march in Washington for civil rights sponsored by the National Association for the Advancement of Colored People ("NAACP"), I was told that the NAACP was a "communist front" organization.

As a result of these activities, the president and dean of Brooklyn College declined to write letters of recommendation for me to law school. Some called me a "fellow traveler" or "pinko."

During the Vietnam War, I organized and taught, at Harvard Law School, the first course in the nation on legal and constitutional issues

---

6 Thomas B. Edsall, "Covid-19 Is Twisting 2020 Beyond All Recognition." *The New York Times*, April 1, 2020.

growing out of our involvement in that undeclared war, with its selective draft that unfairly targeted war protestors. I represented draft resisters, protesters, and civil disobedients. For these activities, I was labeled "unpatriotic" and there were calls for me to be fired.

When Richard Nixon was being investigated for impeachment, I served on the National Board of the American Civil Liberties Union ("ACLU"). Though I personally favored his impeachment for the many high crimes he committed, I opposed some of the tactics being used against him by prosecutors, especially naming him as an unindicted co-conspirator along with some of his indicted subordinates. An unindicted co-conspirator does not have the right to challenge that designation or to be vindicated by a trial. I also opposed the ACLU formally taking a position in favor of Nixon's impeachment, worried that this would compromise its political neutrality. Because I advocated for Nixon's rights, I was called a "turncoat" by some of my Harvard colleagues, who were furious—as I was—at Nixon for firing Archibald Cox, the independent counsel, who was a Harvard colleague.

As part of the O.J. Simpson defense team, I was vilified for helping an accused double murderer escape justice. Strangers sent letters; one included a copy of my book, *Chutzpah*, with a swastika drawn on the cover. A dentist wrote a note on his prescription pad prescribing "a slit throat" for my mother.

I testified against the impeachment of Bill Clinton, consulted with the President and his lawyers on constitutional issues, and appeared on TV opposing his impeachment on the ground that the alleged crime that was at the center of the charges against him was a "low" private crime not a "high" public one. I was attacked by Republican members of Congress and the right-wing media—including some who now praise me—for trivializing perjury and undercutting the rule of law.

When the 2000 presidential election was deadlocked, I went to Florida, where I represented residents of Palm Beach who tried to vote for Al Gore but had inadvertently voted for Patrick Buchanan because of the confusing and illegal "butterfly ballot." When the Supreme Court stopped the recount and handed the election to George W. Bush, I wrote an angry book entitled *Supreme Injustices: How the High Court Hijacked Election 2000*. I was roundly criticized by many in academia, as well as by Justices Sandra Day O'Connor and Antonin Scalia, for questioning the motives of the Justices, who I argued did not pass the "shoe on the other foot test."

My opposition to the invasion of Iraq once again generated accusations that I was unpatriotic. My support following 9/11 for torture warrants and targeted killings of terrorist leaders led some to accuse me of being *too* patriotic and of prioritizing security over civil liberties.[7]

My liberal centrism with regard to the Israeli-Palestinian conflict—I favor a two-state solution that protects Israel's security—has made me enemies on both sides, and my appearances on university campuses are greeted with efforts, from the hard-left, to shut me down and "deplatform" me.

A demonstrably false, and disproven accusation against me by an alleged victim of Jeffrey Epstein has led to lawsuits and efforts to "cancel" my career by hard-left students and other activists, despite the indisputable evidence that I never even met the false accuser.[8]

As a result of being the focus of harsh criticism for the controversial positions I have espoused for more than sixty years, I have developed a thick skin, even in the face of unfair attacks. But until I began to defend the constitutional rights of Donald Trump—a candidate against whom I voted and a President against many of whose policies and actions I have publicly railed—I could not even imagine the hailstorm of condemnation, demonization, threats, and hatred that would be directed at me and my family by strangers, old friends, and even some relatives. People I've known for decades—whose children I bailed out of jail, for whom I wrote college recommendations, helped them and their family members with legal problems—turned viciously against me, refusing to be in the same room, walking out of events if my wife and I appeared, and turning other people against us. One self-righteous lawyer—who had begged me to refer cases or work with him to help his faltering practice—decided that we could "no longer

---

7 See Alan Dershowitz, "The Case for Torture Warrants," *Reuters*, Sept. 7, 2011. I oppose all forms of torture, but I believe it will, in fact, be used in emergency situations, and if it is used, I want due process to prevent its excessive use.

8 See, Alan Dershowitz. *Guilt by Accusation: The Challenge of Proving Innocence in the Age of #MeToo.* (New York: Skyhorse Publishing, 2019).

share each other's society," because any defense of Trump's constitutional rights was "repugnant." The difference is that with earlier controversies, people condemned *what I did*. With controversies regarding President Trump, they condemn and demonize *who I am*. But I *am* what I have always *been*: A principled liberal who puts civil liberties before partisanship. That is not enough for those who believe that I have taken Trump's *side*, rather than the side of the Constitution and civil liberties.[9] It is a sign of the times—of our malignant divisiveness and growing intolerance for political and ideological diversity.

Our divisiveness is not entirely a result of the Trump presidency and the reaction to it. Even before Donald Trump announced his candidacy, our universities—which are the breeding ground for future opinion makers, and political leaders—were fractured by identity politics, intersectionality, "cancel culture," attacks on free speech and due process, propagandized classrooms, anti-Zionism that sometimes morphs into anti-Semitism, intolerance toward evangelical Christianity and social conservatism, demands to check white privilege, and other forms of political correctness that divide rather than unite and that drive ideology toward irreconcilable extremes. Reasoned debates on campus have been replaced by shouting matches, slogan-chanting, cancellation of speeches, demands for safe spaces, firing of politically incorrect faculty, and even violence. The claim of "feeling unsafe" has become a justification for selective, patronizing censorship.

Nor is it likely that our divisiveness would suddenly end if a centrist Democrat such as Joe Biden were to be elected President. The election of a liberal like Biden— although he, like prior centrist candidate Hilary Clinton, eschews the liberal label—would represent the *temporary* victory of old, establishment centrist Democrats over younger, more radical extremists who may well represent the future. One critic characterizes Biden as "a placeholder candidate, a man who offers no new ideas and mainly talks about the past." I have a more positive view of Biden, but I don't believe he represents the future of the Democratic

---

9 See, e.g., Nancy Gertner, "Alan Dershowitz Used to be an Icon for Civil Liberties. What Happened?" WBUR Cognoscenti, January 28, 2020; Evan Mandery, "What Happened to Alan Dershowitz?" *Politico*, May 11, 2018.

Party. Biden himself seems to understand this. In order to secure the endorsement of Senators Sanders and Warren, Biden accepted several of their proposals that were considerably to the left of what he and President Obama had supported. He had little choice because Obama himself has, according to a *New York Times* headline "pivot[ed] left":

> Obama went out of his way to signal that he agrees with the party's shift toward a more progressive agenda. "I could not be prouder of the incredible progress that we made together during my presidency," he said. "But if I were running today I wouldn't run the same race or have the same platform as I did in 2008. The world is different."[10]

Bernie Sanders, who—according to *The New York Times* —"almost single-handedly moved the Democratic Party to the left," has now been "elevated" to the role of "standard-bearer of American liberalism and the leader of a self-styled political revolution."[11] The very fact that the *Times* characterized a self-described "Democratic Socialist" as the standard-bearer of American "*liberalism*" shows how far left the center has moved.

We are in danger of losing our identity as a nation of centrist liberals and conservatives who talk to and argue with our counterparts, as I used to with William F. Buckley. Debate is being replaced with demonization. Ideas matter less than identity. Disagreements are resolved by shouting louder than the other side, trying to prevent them from speaking, or walking out when they do speak. We are quickly becoming a nation of extremists, of warring camps of far-left radicals and far-right reactionaries—of Trump haters and Trump lovers. Classic liberals and conservatives—who place the values of speech, due process, and basic liberties *above* partisan results—are in the process of turning into endangered species, replaced by zealots who know "The Truth" and see no need for opposing views or due process. Zealots are *never*

10 David Leonhardt, "Obama Pivots Left," *The New York Times*, April 15, 2020.

11 Sydney Ember, "Where the Promise of Bernie Sanders Goes Now." *The New York Times*, April 8, 2020.

mistaken. Their opponents are *always mistaken*. There is no place for nuance, doubt or compromise. Purity and certainty are demanded. The spirit of healthy skepticism—which is the spirit of liberty and of true liberalism and conservatism—is incompatible with the comfortable certainty of self-righteousness, a comfortableness that is confirmed by niche media that tell viewers and readers what they already know and what they want to hear. We no longer respect the caution of Cromwell, who famously said, "I beseech you, in the bowels of Christ, think it possible that you may be mistaken." To invoke a religious analogy, the political world is now sharply divided into true believers and atheists, with no room for agnostics or skeptics.

The liberal tradition in America is on life-support, and with it the center left and center right. Democrats in the tradition of Roosevelt, Kennedy, Johnson, Humphrey, Scoop Jackson, Moynihan, and Clinton are becoming as anachronistic as Republicans in the tradition of Rockefeller, Javits, and Eisenhower.

Being a centrist, liberal, civil libertarian who puts principle over partisanship—which is what I try to be—means that I cannot identify with the hard-left trend of the Democratic Party. But nor can I join the socially and religiously extremist right wing of the Republican Party. I find myself politically homeless in the current illiberal and partisan landscape. The hard-left has left me because of intolerance for free speech and due process, and because of its knee-jerk opposition to Israel and Western values; the hard-right is not open to me because of its policies toward gay rights, a woman's right to choose, the environment, separation of church and state, and other social issues; the liberal civil liberties center, which remains my chosen home, is shrinking to oblivion, as is the conservative civil liberties center. To be sure, there are still some pundits and politicians who adhere to centrist liberalism or conservatism, but their numbers and visibility are shrinking, and their reasoned voices are being drowned out by the noisy extremists on both sides.

Nor are there compelling explanations or justifications for this movement away from the center. In previous eras of deep divisiveness—for example, during the early 1930s, when much of Europe was largely divided between Fascism and Communism—the world was experiencing a cataclysmic depression, with massive unemployment and displacements. We are experiencing nothing comparable today, even in the face of the Coronavirus, and the economic and social crises it has generated.

Moreover, our current divisiveness *preceded* the current public health crisis and is unlikely to end with its resolution. People are angry, but the reasons for their anger are not easily discernable on economic or other material grounds. The conflicts we are experiencing—over income inequality, climate control, racial injustice, gender inequality immigration, and other important issues—have been with us for a long time and require the sort of nuanced compromises, particularly about means, that are becoming more difficult to achieve. They do not explain the extreme divisiveness or anger we are now experiencing, and which have been increasingly evident over the last several years.

But the lack of material explanations does not negate the reality of the divisive anger, which is palpable. Nor does it assure us that our deep divisions—which are, in part, generational, racial, gender, religious, ideological, and political—would end with the election of a new president. The reality is that the lack of discourse has cemented these divisions, and unless we restore dialogue and compromise, they will be with us for a long time.

The other indisputable reality is that our nation, and the world, does better for its citizens when governing from the center than from the extremes. Neither the brown of Fascism nor the red of Communism have proven beneficial to the world. As a Jewish-American, I am especially concerned with current trends toward extremism, because Jews have historically suffered from both the brown and the red. Today, Jews are physically attacked more by right-wing anti-Semites and Muslim extremists, but they are marginalized and demonized by the anti-Israel hard-left. The dangers from the hard-left are far more prevalent on university campuses—where our future leaders are educated—so they may reflect the future, whereas the current serious threats from the hard-right may reflect more of the past. Also, as a professor for half a century, I am personally more familiar with the increasing influence of the hard-left. And as a liberal, I feel an obligation to focus more on the dangers of the hard-left, leaving it to my conservative colleagues to call out the evils of the hard-right. Both extremes pose their own, sometimes overlapping, dangers to America's long tradition of centrism.

Centrist liberalism and conservatism have produced far better results, not only for Jews, but for everyone, as judged by any realistic standards. There may be a time and place for extremism: slavery called for extreme remedial measures, including a civil war. But this is neither the time nor place for the kind of thoughtless, uncompromising extremism that is now plaguing our world.

Our nation's historic commitment to centrism has accorded us competitive advantages against other nations that have suffered from both right- and left-wing extremism and wide swings of the political pendulum. We are at risk of losing that advantage.

This book is an attempt to revitalize the liberal center and to make the case for dialogue and due process. It is also an effort to describe the current dilemma faced by so many who, like me, feel abandoned by what seems like an inexorable movement toward extremism and away from the values of tolerance, open-mindedness, and fairness that have been the hallmarks of classic liberalism and conservatism for most of my lifetime. It begins with an effort to define and describe the essence of liberalism.

CHAPTER 1

What Is Liberalism?

I am a liberal. And so, I believe, are many other people who currently refuse to define themselves by the word "liberal"—a term that is currently being demonized not only by the hard-right, but also by the hard-left, and even by centrist politicians who fear the fate of liberals of the past. If more people understood what it really means to be a liberal, many who today call themselves "progressives" or even "radicals" would proudly proclaim their liberalism. So would some centrist conservatives.

There is, of course, no agreed-upon dictionary definition of the word liberal,[12] any more than there is of progressive, radical, leftist, or even conservative. But there is, I believe, a common understanding of some characteristics that are more closely associated with liberals than with other groupings.

I define a liberal as a person who is tolerant of other ideas,[13]

---

12 The Oxford dictionary defines "liberal" as: willing to understand and respect other people's behaviour, opinions, etc., especially when they are different from your own; believing people should be able to choose how they behave. https://www.oxfordlearnersdictionaries.com/us/definition/english/liberal_1.

13 I use the world "tolerant" not in the negative way George Washington used it in his famous letter to the Hebrew Conservation of Newport on August 18, 1790 in which he said: "It is now no more that toleration is spoken of as if it were the indulgence of one class of people that another enjoyed the exercise of their inherent natural rights, for,

open-minded, willing to consider change, open to criticism, welcoming of dialogue, free-thinking, unprejudiced, reformist, not bound by tradition, intellectually curious, and generous. A liberal is skeptical of all orthodoxies and rigid traditions—whether religious or secular—and insists on the right and need to think for one's self and to learn from experience, from others, and from science. A liberal eschews extremes and understands nuance and the need to strike balances among conflicting rights and between ideology and pragmatism. A liberal understands that the democratic process doesn't guarantee liberal outcomes, but requires compromise. A liberal treasures true diversity of ideas, backgrounds and cultures, not limited to race, ethnicity, gender, or sexual orientation.

A liberal believes in, advocates, and practices basic civil liberties *for every person*, regardless of whether, or what, *they* believe or do. Liberalism and civil liberties go hand-in-hand. A commitment to universal civil liberties—even for one's ideological opponents—is among the factors that distinguish liberalism from hard-left radicalism.

Some have tried to associate liberalism with youth, as this quote—attributed to Churchill—attests: "Show me a young conservative and I'll show you someone with no heart; show me an old liberal and I'll show you someone with no brain." This, in my view, confuses radicalism with liberalism and conservatism. I know many old liberals with lots of brains, and lots of young conservatives with lots of heart, but not too many old radicals with common sense, or young reactionaries with a spirit of generosity. I also know many—far too many—young hard-left radicals who are anything but liberal: they reject freedom of speech, tolerance for opposing viewpoints, open-mindedness, and a sense of humor. And I know many old reactionaries who have stopped thinking. Age has little to do with political ideology, except that many young people often place a lower value on nuance and compromise than do many older people.

Many of the characteristics of both young and old liberals are also

---

happily, the Government of the United States, which gives to bigotry no sanction, to persecution no assistance, requires only that they who live under its protection should demean themselves as good citizens in giving it on all occasions their effectual support."

shared by principled conservatives of every age. What thinking person would not want to be known as tolerant, open-minded, unprejudiced, nuanced, and willing to consider change? What, then, distinguishes my liberalism from the conservatism of friends and colleagues whom I admire?

Liberalism goes beyond personal characteristics. It includes political, economic and ideological components as well. These components are harder to define than to identify. To quote Justice Potter Steward's judicial attempt to define "hard-core pornography": "I shall not today attempt further to define it and perhaps I could never succeed in intelligibly doing so. But I know it when I see it, and the motion picture involved in this case is not that."[14]

I, too, know a liberal—or even more clearly an illiberal, whether of the right or left—when I see, hear, or read one, even if I cannot define with precision all of the elements that comprise that elusive and dynamic term. Some of these political and ideological elements are, however, possible to identify.

They include an effort to move toward greater equality—economic, political, educational, medical, and legal—without denying real differences and without imposing rigid restrictions that prevent reasonable differentials in outcomes based on free market principles.[15] We support equality of opportunity but not necessarily of outcome. We want today's enormous gap between the super-rich and the poor working classes narrowed, not because the rich are too rich, but because the poor are too poor in a society as wealthy as ours. We believe in true meritocracy, where everyone has a fair chance to succeed, and where hard work and talent are rewarded. A true liberal rejects the Marxist mantra: "From each according to his ability, to each according to his

---

14 Jacobellis v. Ohio, 378 U.S. 184 (1964). I was a law clerk at the time of this decision and helped draft Justice Goldberg's concurring opinion.

15 For a brilliant satire on the quest for total equality of outcome, see Kurt Vonnegut's short story, "Harrison Bergeron", which begins: "The year was 2081, and everybody was finally equal. They weren't only equal before God and the law. They were equal every which way. Nobody was smarter than anybody else. Nobody was better looking than anybody else. Nobody was stronger or quicker than anybody else. All this equality was due to the 211th, 212th, and 213th amendments to the Constitution and to the unceasing vigilance of agents of the United States Handicapper General."

needs," because that simplistic formula refuses to recognize real differences based on individual decisions to prioritize productivity over pleasure. The liberal perspective supports progressive taxation ("according to ability") and an economic and medical safety net for all ("according to need"), but it also rewards hard work, ability, innovation, and success, without demanding that social goods be distributed by government bureaucracies solely in accord with a rigid need formula. A floor is different from a ceiling, and liberals believe there should be a floor below which no one should be permitted to fall, but no ceiling—or a ceiling high enough to incentivize innovation—limiting where a person may reach.

A telling example of an important difference between liberalism and radicalism is in the manner by which Bernie Sanders, a Democratic Socialist, speaks about the pharmacological industry, and how differently many liberals regard it. Sanders demonized "Big Pharma" for its "profiteering", without acknowledging that it is the profit motive that incentivizes the remarkable life-saving pharmacological innovations in which free-market countries, such as the U.S. and Israel, lead the world. Moreover, the profits of Big Pharma are shared among its stockholders, many of whom are working- and middle-class pension and fund beneficiaries. The Coronavirus pandemic has seen some pharmaceutical companies eschewing profits in favor of helping address this crisis. A liberal critique of the pharmacological industry would focus on the excessive profits of some executives, the high cost of needed drugs, the exploitive marketing of certain products, the refusal to develop necessary pharmaceuticals that might not be sufficiently profitable—while at the same time recognizing the enormous good many Big Pharma companies have done, and without destroying incentives to innovation.

Liberals reject open-admission programs to colleges and universities that ignore proven competence in favor of rigid equality of outcome, while insisting that all applicants be accorded realistic opportunities to receive educational and vocational resources compatible with their abilities. A principled liberal should be conflicted about race-based affirmative action programs whose end is greater equality, but whose means require unequal treatment based on race.[16] A liberal,

16 See Justice William O. Douglas' opinion in the *DeFunis* case, 416 U.S. 312, (1974)

as distinguished from a radical, cares about means as well as ends, and seeks to strike appropriate balances between the two.

A recent critic of liberalism confuses liberalism with radicalism when he says that "modern American liberals" do not believe "fully in the greatest of all liberal principles—equality. Affirmative action, political correctness, identity politics—each affirms the belief that some citizens, have rights that others don't."[17] Liberals share the radical goal of equality but are often conflicted about the means for achieving it.

A liberal accepts basic principles of civil liberties, such as due process and concern for the rights of those accused of crimes, even the most heinous and illiberal of crimes, such as hate-crimes committed by racists. A liberal recognizes that enforcing the rights of those accused and convicted of crimes will result in some guilty and dangerous criminals going free. But it is a price we are required to pay, within reason, to assure that our criminal justice system remains fair and committed to the principle that it is "better that ten guilty go free than one innocent be wrongly convicted." That heavy price—a price that we recognize falls unequally on the poor and powerless—must also be paid to avoid undue intrusions by government on rights of privacy,[18] bodily integrity, and counsel. We recognize the centrality of these and other basic rights to the rule of law, while also recognizing that they sometimes need to be balanced against the needs of society to protect vulnerable citizens against predation.

Most liberals support the goals of the "Me Too" movement, while also recognizing the need for due process for those accused of sexual misconduct. There is inevitably some disagreement among liberals about priorities and how to strike the appropriate balance with regard to evidentiary standards and procedural safeguards.[19]

Most liberals oppose capital punishment, torture, and other forms of unnecessarily "cruel and unusual punishment." We are concerned with

---

at 1708. See my article in *Cardozo Law Review*: Alan M. Dershowitz & Laura Hanft, "Affirmative Action and the Harvard College Diversity-Discretion Model: Paradigm or Pretext," 1 Cardozo L. Rev. 379 (1979).

17 See supra note 1.

18 See my debate with Professor Kahan in *Shouting Fire*, (New York: Little Brown, 2002), pp. 74-78.

19 Dershowitz, *Guilt by Accusation*.

the overuse of deadly force by police, while recognizing the pressures under which police operate. We refuse to demonize all police officers and insist that they, too, are entitled to due process and the presumption of innocence when accused of misconduct. We support striking appropriate balances among the needs for effective law enforcement, equal treatment based on race and class, privacy, and due process.

We recognize that currently there are differences in violent crime rates based on race, poverty, family cohesion, and other factors. We seek to address this problem in a rational manner without exacerbating racial tensions or denying the reality that race is a factor that cuts in different directions in our criminal justice system. We categorically reject any notion that crime is in any way related to race in a genetic manner, recalling that bigots throughout history have sought to attribute criminal tendencies to Jews, Italians, Irish, Romani, Slavs, Mexicans, Muslims, and other ethnic, racial and religious groups.

We oppose over-criminalization, over-confinement, draconian mandatory minimum sentences, and racial and class discrimination in the enforcement of criminal justice, but we don't want to empty our prisons, open all jail doors, or allow all manner of abuse excuses based on poverty, upbringing, or cultural differences. We believe that criminal and other punitive statutes be written clearly and interpreted narrowly, so as to avoid giving too much discretion to law enforcement. We support efforts to de-institutionalize older, non-violent inmates who are at risk of highly contagious viruses, such as Coronavirus.

Liberals support reasonable gun control, while recognizing that the Second Amendment has been interpreted by the Supreme Court to accord individuals the right to own weapons for self-defense, hunting and sport. Many liberals would have preferred if the Founders had not included a Second Amendment, but are unwilling to tamper with the Bill of Rights. We believe that the words "well-regulated" in the context of the first clause of the Amendment provides a textual basis for effective gun regulation.[20]

A true liberal values freedom of expression, while recognizing that

20 The second Amendment states: "A well-regulated militia, being necessary to the security of a free state, the right of the people to keep and bear arms, shall not be infringed."

speech—especially hate speech and speech that deeply offends—is anything but "free." Words can hurt, but so can censorship. We reject the notion, reflected in a ditty of our youth, that "sticks and stones may break your bones but words will never harm you." We understand that words, uttered by bullies and bigots, can hurt as much as stones. But we also understand what Sigmund Freud meant when he said, "The first human who hurled an insult instead of a stone was the founder of civilization." We err on the side of more speech and less censorship, even for ideas and images that we find repulsive or dangerous. We reject "safe spaces" to protect against offensive expression and look to the open marketplace of ideas—rather than the office of the censor—as the place to counter bad speech, while recognizing that the marketplace is an imperfect mechanism for producing truth, especially in the age of social media, cable TV, and other sources of biased information that goes viral. Like democracy itself, freedom of speech may be the worst approach except for all the others that have been tried over time.

The alternative to freedom of speech is censorship by governments, universities, and other institutions, and history has demonstrated the danger of allocating the power to suppress the expression of ideas to such entities. We loathe "political correctness," remembering that this seductive phrase grew out of the Stalinist purges of those who deviated from the correct political line established by the Kremlin for all things political, economic, artistic, cultural, or ideological.[21] We also remember that in the 1940s and 1950s, it was the right, not the left, that censored political speech through blacklisting, red channels, and other McCarthyite programs. Today it is largely the hard-left that advocates and practices "deplatforming," "cancelling," and other forms of direct and indirect censorship. We accept our Supreme Court's response to censorship from the left and right alike: "Under the First Amendment, there is no such thing as a false idea. However pernicious an opinion may seem, we depend for its correction not on the

21 Angelo Codevilla, Professor Emeritus of International Relations at Boston College, addresses Stalin's use of this phrase: "The notion of political correctness came into use among Communists in the 1930s as a semi-humorous reminder that the Party's interest is to be treated as a reality that ranks above reality itself." "The Rise of Political Correctness," *Claremont Review of Books*, Fall 2016.

conscience of judges or juries, but on the competition of other ideas."[22] Liberals are conflicted about whether political contributions—especially by large corporations—should be considered protected speech. We disapprove of the impact of big money on elections, but we support an expansive definition of political expression that includes political contributions—at least by individuals. Many of us think the Supreme Court has gone too far in protecting the rights of corporations in the political process, while not going far enough in protecting the rights of individual voters, especially among minorities and the poor.

Liberals believe in a "living" Constitution and an activist Supreme Court. We recognize and understand that some provisions of our Constitution are "dead" in the sense they are not subject to interpretation—such as the age qualifications of holding office. We also understand that judicial activism is a double-edged sword that can be used by judicial conservatives to strike down liberal legislation, as was done during the New Deal, and is being done now with regard to gun control and campaign finance reform. As Justice Scalia once wrote me, "You may yet conclude that originalism is the safest course."[23] I, along with most other liberals, do not agree, recalling the enormous gains to civil rights and liberties brought about by the activist Warren court. We understand the risks of judicial activism, and we agree that in a democracy, important policy choices should generally be left to the legislature, subject to checks and balances by the other branches.

Most liberals recognize that the power of the executive branch has grown considerably since the Constitution was ratified. We understand the need for presidential authority in an age of instantaneous communications, international terrorism, life-threatening pandemics, pressing policy demands in a complex and ever-changing world, a sprawling bureaucracy, and legislative gridlock. But we are concerned with the impact of the imperial presidency on our system of separation of powers and checks and balances. That is among the reasons we

---

22 *Gertz v. Robert Welch*, 418 U.S. 323 (1974).

23 *See* Alan Dershowitz. *Taking the Stand.* (New York: Broadway Books, 2013), pp. 271-272.

favor a more activist judiciary: to serve as a check on presidential (and legislative) over-reaching.

We disagree about whether the constitutional criteria for impeaching and removing a president is "living" or "dead" and whether the words "other high crimes and misdemeanors" are flexible enough to include "abuse of power" or other non-criminal criteria. In the recent effort to remove President Trump, my view—that criminal-like behavior akin to treason and bribery is required for impeachment[24]—was clearly in the minority among liberals, though I believe it would have been more widely accepted if Hillary Clinton had been elected and were impeached for "abuse of power." Most liberals, who took an expansive view of the criteria for removal when President Trump was impeached, took a far narrower view of the criteria when President Bill Clinton was impeached.

Liberals are understandably conflicted about big government. We recognize that it requires large governmental bureaucracies to help the poor, the disenfranchised, the elderly, the young, the ill, and others in need of services, such as veterans. But we worry about big institutions, especially, but not exclusively, governmental bureaucracies. We recognize that bigness can be both a curse and a blessing, and we see the need to strike an appropriate balance between the virtues and vices of big government, insisting that there be checks and balances in place to control the dangers of big brother and sister. We echo Justice Brandeis's warning about "The curse of bigness,"[25] and we are concerned about the increasing power of unregulated social media, but also fear the First Amendment implications of the heavy hand of governmental censorship over private media.

A liberal insists on strict separation between church and state and in limiting the influence of formal religions on governance. We fear the combined power of churches and governmental institutions and believe that history has vindicated our concerns. It is precisely because we have separated religion from governance that our citizens attend church, synagogue, and mosque more frequently than citizens of other

---

24 See Dershowitz, *Defending the Constitution.*

25 See Louis D. Brandeis, "A Curse of Bigness," *Harper's Weekly*, Jan. 10, 1914, p. 18.

Western democracies. We insist on the right to criticize religious institutions and teachings, as well as those of the state and other powerful institutions. Although many liberals are personally religious, we believe that the rule of law and the principles of democracy, rather than the word of God, should govern our public lives. We also recognize that individuals who believe that their private lives should be governed by their God have that right, as long as it does not intrude on the rights of others. We support reasonable accommodations that strike a proper balance between the free exercise of religion and government neutrality toward religious and non-religious beliefs. We believe that in striking that delicate balance, governments should be empowered to override religious objections to compelling public health measures—such as mandatory vaccinations and reasonable quarantines—designed to prevent the spread of deadly contagious diseases. We deplore the hypocrisy of those who claim to be speaking in the name of God, while rejecting some of the most uplifting aspects of their own religions.

Liberals believe in basing policies on the best scientific, economic, and other fact-based research. Though we are skeptical of all orthodoxies, including scientific ones—we remember the excesses of genetics in the 1920s, 1930s, and 1940s[26]—we reject the kind of pseudo-science that denies climate change, evolution, the efficacy of vaccinations, the spread of viruses, and other proven, if ever-changing, scientific consensuses. We place reason and experience above faith and dogma.

Liberals believe that the classrooms of public schools and universities should not be used to inculcate religious or political views. Religious conservatives want God and Jesus in the classrooms, while radical leftists want Marx and Arafat in the classroom. We defend the right to preach and proselytize outside the classroom, but not to captive students in the classroom. We believe that it is the proper role of the professor to teach students *how* to think, not to propagandize them about *what* to think.

Liberals value personal privacy, especially at a time when many young people seem prepared to expose their most private thoughts, actions, and relationships through social media, while many older folks

---

26 See *Buck v. Bell*. 274 U.S. 200 (1927).

are willing to surrender their privacy in the name of increased security. While recognizing the legitimate need of government to gather relevant information to thwart terrorism, contagious diseases, and other dangers, liberals demand process—such as the warrant requirements of the Fourth Amendment—as well as accountability and evidence that the benefits of the intrusions outweigh their cost.[27] We recognize that emerging technologies can protect our privacy as well as intrude upon it, and we demand democratic accountability from both private and governmental institutions that impact our private lives.

Liberals believe that governments should not dictate our private actions, unless these actions have discernible effects on others. We generally accept, with varying interpretations, the principle stated by John Stuart Mill: "That the only purpose for which power can be rightfully exercised over any member of a civilized community, against his will, is to prevent harm to others. His own good, either physical or moral, is not a sufficient warrant." More on Mill's enormous contributions to the philosophy of liberalism in chapter 3.

This issue of government compulsion to help oneself is complex morally, economically, and politically. Since "no man is an island," government—that means citizens—must pay for much harm individuals do to themselves. Similarly, adults may have the right to refuse medical treatment that would benefit only them, but not vaccinations that prevent the spread of diseases to others. We accept the reality that during pandemics, other liberal or libertarian rights may have to be compromised in the interest of public health, but we insist that any such limitations be as narrow as reasonable and limited in time. Extremists on both the hard-right and hard-left try to exploit pandemics such as the Coronavirus to make ideological points regarding the role of government, business, science, and the media.[28]

Benevolent state compulsion pits certain liberal principles against other liberal principles. Reasonable liberals can and do disagree about how to prioritize and calibrate these conflicting principles. Indeed,

---

27 See Alan Dershowitz, "Is there a Right to Anonymity for Coronavirus Carriers in the U.S." *The Hill*, March 18, 2020.

28 See Alan Dershowitz, "Exploiting Pandemic for Ideological Advantage is Wrong." *Newsmax* April 10, 2020.

it is fair to say that liberals, more than others, often find the need to balance conflicting principles, because they believe that principles are not absolute or God-given, but rather are feeble human efforts to live by just, decent, but imperfect human rules.

Liberals also recognize that democracy is messy. As Churchill famously put it: "It is the worst form of government, except for all those other forms that have been tried from time to time." To work, democracy often needs compromise—sometimes principled, others less so—and most liberals are not purists when compromise promises a better outcome than rigid adherence to singular principles. As Barney Frank, who personified liberalism during his many years in Congress, used to ask of every piece of imperfect legislation that he was asked to vote on: "Compared to what?" A liberal understands that in a democracy, one cannot always get his or her first choice, and that if the second choice is better than the third or fourth choice, then the "Compared to what?" test would mandate accepting the second choice. The "least worst" may be the best we can do in some circumstances.

Liberals acknowledge that rights may sometimes clash with other rights and that prioritizing one over another may be necessary. Consider for example, the difference between laws (thankfully now deemed unconstitutional) that prohibited gay sex and laws that criminalized abortion: gay sex hurts no one, while abortion destroys (kills) a fetus (a potential human being). A liberal should have no ambivalence about opposing laws criminalizing gay sex or prohibiting gay marriage, but some ambivalence about laws permitting abortion, especially in late term.[29] The former requires no striking of balance, since liberals believe that one person's religious or moral views should not be imposed by law on others, while the latter requires that we prefer the mothers' choice over the alleged "right" of a potential human to be born. Liberals recognize that the fetus is a potential life that the law has an interest in protecting, at least under certain circumstances. We would agree with laws that punish the deliberate

29 See Cathryn Donohoe. "To be Liberal and pro-Life: Nat Hentoff, Champion of 'Inconvenient Life." *The Washington Times*, November 6, 1989, for a description of a liberal who opposes abortion.

harming of a fetus. We support prenatal care and agree with Barney Frank's critique of some religious fundamentalists, who believe the government's interest in the fetus "begins at conception and ends at birth." But we also recognize that a pregnant woman or girl has a compelling interest in her bodily integrity and in terminating an unwanted or dangerous pregnancy. Most liberals strike that difficult balance in favor of the woman's right to choose, though some give more weight than others to the right of the fetus, especially if it has reached the stage of viability. Many liberals are and should be conflicted over the power of the State to demand that pregnant women not smoke, drink to excess, or engage in other activities that may endanger the fetus, which they intend to birth.

Balance must also be struck with regard to laws criminalizing some drugs and some forms of violent pornography, especially if evidence were to show causal links to abusive behavior or violent crime. Life and law are complex, and liberals do not seek to deny the complexity that must be acknowledged when we seek to impose rules to govern human conduct. We recognize the difficulty of proving such causal links and insist that in situations where proof is uncertain, doubts should generally be resolved in favor of liberty and individual choice.[30]

There is no real consensus on a liberal view of foreign policy, except that many liberals tend to be more "dovish" than many conservatives. There is, of course, a strain of isolationism among some conservatives: recall the election of 1940, in which liberal Democrats were more willing to enter the war against Hitler than were isolationist Republicans. But in subsequent military actions—against Communist and Muslim enemies—liberals have protested, though some have supported our government. Some contemporary Republican isolationists, such as Senator Rand Paul, have also objected, though their numbers and influence are relatively small.

Liberals today are divided about our policies with regard to Israel, with most supporting Israel's right to defend its citizens against external and internal threats, but with many critical of Israel's long occupation

30 See Dershowitz, *Shouting Fire*, pp. 163-175.

and settlement policies.[31] There were sharp divisions among liberal Democrats over the nuclear deal struck with Iran in 2015, while nearly all conservative Republicans opposed the deal as too favorable to Iran. Many liberals believed we could have gotten a better deal, but refused to oppose the deal on the table because, in their view, it was "less bad" than the alternatives and therefore passed the "Compared to what?" test. Some liberals, such as Senator Charles Schumer and me, thought it failed that test. And there are current disagreements about proposed courses of action in Syria and areas in which foreign terrorist groups are operating, as well as the right approach to preventing foreign-inspired domestic terrorism. There is also considerable disagreement about policies regarding regime change. We hate repressive, authoritarian tyrants, but we recognize that the alternative to domestic tyranny may be exported terrorism;[32] so once again, the liberal question regarding the evils of incumbent dictators is "compared to what?" or "to whom?"

Again, Liberals understand that there are no perfect solutions to these complex national security issues and that balance must be struck and transparent processes implemented and followed. Liberals are also sensitive to the relationship between national security and civil liberties, recognizing the historical reality that domestic liberty is often the first casualty of war.

Liberalism is as much an attitude and temperament as it is a policy or agenda, though it partakes in both. We know liberalism when we see it, and tragically we are seeing too little of it today. We also know illiberalism when we see it, and frighteningly, we are seeing too much of it today, especially among young people on the left. We also understand that liberalism and illiberalism may reflect upbringing, experience, and peer pressure. In the next chapter, we explore the sources of liberalism.

---

31 See Sam Stein, "Biden Embraces Endorsement of Liberal Jewish Group JStreet." *Daily Beast*, April 17, 2020.

32 The end of the Shah's rule in Iran led to the current regime, which is the largest exporter of terrorism in the world.

CHAPTER 2

I Was Born a Liberal and Will Die a Liberal

Philosophy is often autobiography.[33] Where one stands is a product of where one sat, whom one sat next to, and whom one listened to growing up. Sometimes a person's philosophy is a reaction to her upbringing, but only rarely is upbringing irrelevant to whether a person becomes—as an adult—a liberal, conservative, or something else. For several years, I taught a freshman seminar at Harvard College entitled, "Where Does Your Morality Come From?" The philosophical views of these eighteen-year-old students were largely shaped by parents, peers, teachers, religious leaders, and others they encountered during their upbringing. Their ideology did not spring, fully formed, by some instantaneous epiphany, though ideas can change quite dramatically, with new experiences, peers, and teachers, as they often do during one's college years.

I was born a liberal. I know no other way, having been raised by a typical liberal Jewish Brooklyn family, in the Borough Park neighborhood of Brooklyn during the post-World War II era. Our political heroes were FDR, Harry Truman, Adlai Stevenson, Hubert Humphrey, Robert Wagner, Jacob Javits, and Fiorello La Guardia. Our sports

33 Ralph Waldo Emerson observed: "There is properly no history, only biography."

heroes were Jackie Robinson, Joe Louis, Allie Sherman, and later, Sandy Koufax.

We hated Joseph McCarthy and Roy Cohn, but we also despised Stalin and the American Communist Party. We supported desegregation, opposed capital punishment, and contributed to the ACLU. We generally voted for Democrats, but sometimes for liberal Republicans, such as Jacob Javits.

We were proud to be called "liberals." We were the "good guys"—the ones who cared about others and about preserving liberties. The conservatives were the bad guys—selfish, ungenerous, and unconcerned about the rights of others.

We didn't debate the finer points of what exactly it meant to *be* a liberal; our *actions* defined our liberalism. We marched for civil rights. But we respected the police, whom we knew through their Police Athletic League (PAL) programs. We opposed blacklists, red channels, and all forms of censorship, though we had little sympathy for actual "reds" or "pink" fellow travelers. We were told to stay away from the tiny, dusty bookstore that was owned by an admirer of Leon Trotsky and sold "subversive" books, though our curiosity drove us to defy that directive and sneak into the store to taste its forbidden fruits. None of us were converted, any more than we were converted by some of our illiberal rabbis. We had doubts about the Korean War, and we were worried about a nuclear attack from the Soviet Union, especially when our teachers made us practice hiding under our desks in what were called "duck and cover drills." When we got a bit older, we opposed the Vietnam War. But we were not conscientious objectors. We just didn't want to be drafted, to fight and possibly die in a war we didn't understand or support. But neither did we want to risk our futures by going to jail or Canada.

We favored liberal immigration policies because our own co-religionists and relatives had been kept out during crucial periods, and some were still trying to come to America.

We knew that certain colleges, corporations, and neighborhoods didn't welcome Jews, Blacks, Catholics, and other non-WASPs, but we sensed that these forms of "polite" bigotry were the last gasp of a dying aristocracy. We were not particularly sensitive to discrimination against gays or women, but nor would we have consciously engaged in overt bigotry against any group. By today's standards, our ignorance and silence regarding these issues would be deserving of criticism, but standards, attitudes, and awareness were different back in the day.

We knew nothing about abortion rights, gay rights, affirmative action, or gun control. We just believed that everyone should be treated fairly, no one should be discriminated against or censored, and that the government was generally our friend. We were appalled when Brooklyn Dodgers slugger Dixie Walker and other bigoted baseball players refused to play on the same team as Jackie Robinson, and we applauded the Dodgers for keeping Robinson and trading Walker. Life was simple in the late 1940s and 1950s, and we took our liberal approach to it for granted.

We were comfortable with our centrist liberalism, which was unchallenged in our neighborhood by competing worldviews. There were a few theoretical socialists in Borough Park, but the abstract nature of their commitment to Marxist equality was best illustrated by the joke about Chayim and Moshe, who had been friends in Poland until Chayim left for New York. Moshe, too, made it to New York a year later, and was greeted by Chayim, who announced, "I've discovered a wonderful new philosophy called 'socialism.'" Moshe asked, "What's that?" Chayim replied, "Socialism means that if I have two houses, I have to give you one of them." "Sounds good," Moshe replied. "It is good," Chayim assured him. "It means if I have two cars, I give you one." "So let me understand," Moshe asked: "If you have two shirts, you have to give me one?" "No, no." Chayim insisted. "Two shirts I have!"

My friends and neighbors had two shirts, but none of us had two houses or cars. We lived frugally and moderately in apartments or in two- or three-family stucco houses. We aspired to attend a New York City College, which was free. We wanted to be doctors, lawyers, dentists, and accountants. The girls in our neighborhood aspired to marry "GEP"s—boys with good earning potential. (I did not qualify.) We didn't want to change the world—just improve it a bit. We didn't know the term "white privilege," and if we had, we would not have seen ourselves as beneficiaries, because as Eastern European Jews, we did not feel privileged in what my mother called "their world." We loved and admired our parents, but we—and they—wanted us to do better than they had done, especially during the Depression. I recall my father once telling me he was thinking of voting for Richard Nixon. I was shocked. Nixon was a Republican whose politics favored the rich, and we weren't rich, I reminded my father. I will always remember his response: "I'm not rich, but I'm hoping you will be, so I'm voting our future, not our past or present." In the end, I don't think my father was actually capable of voting Republican.

We were generally comfortable with our middle of the road liberalism. We knew no other way. We believed that liberalism was part of our cultural, religious, and ethnic heritage. Liberalism was in our self-interest, but it also satisfied our need to be charitable to others. We took seriously the admonition of the Jewish sage Hillel: "If I am not for myself, who will be for me, but if I am for myself alone, what am I?" We voted our vicarious memories and our modest aspirations.

We regarded the few neighbors to the left of us as unrealistic dreamers, and the even fewer to the right as selfish strivers. My Uncle Moishe, whom I loved, was a Republican, although he espoused liberal values. He explained that being a Republican helped his career. I understood. For the rest of us, we were where we should have been on the political and ideological spectrum. We expected to remain there forever. Remarkably, many of us did, despite very different levels of financial success. We were liberals for life! And most of us still are, though our definition of what our liberalism is has probably changed a bit since we moved out of our 1950's shtetl and encountered a wider world.

In addition to being centrist liberals, our other primary identification was as Zionists, who supported the establishment of a Nation State for the Jewish people, especially since the Holocaust (a term we didn't yet know) had murdered and uprooted so many European Jews who were living in displaced persons' camps. Some survivors were living in our neighborhood. Relatives on both sides of our family did not survive.

There was no conflict between our liberalism and our Zionism. Indeed, Zionism was seen as a liberal program—the National Liberation

Movement of the Jewish People. Its leading American proponents—such as Supreme Court Justice Louis Brandeis, Rabbi Stephen S. Wise, Emma Lazarus, and Henrietta Szold—were paragons of centrist liberalism. Even the hard-left, including many Communists, supported Zionism and the establishment of Israel, which they saw as a democratic-socialist island amidst a sea of repressive Arab monarchies and tyrannies. Both the U.S. and the Soviet Union immediately recognized Israel, and Czechoslovakia (then under the control of the Soviet Union) provided arms for the Israeli army. The screenplay for the popular film *Exodus*—based on the equally popular book by Leon Uris—was written by Dalton Trumbo, a writer who had been blacklisted for his membership in the Communist Party. It glorified the establishment of Israel and demonized Israel's Arab enemies. A decade later, Martin Luther King was a strong supporter of the Nation State of the Jewish people.

Israel's opponents were conservative, often anti-Semitic, state department bureaucrats (some of the same ones who stopped Jews from entering the U.S. during the Holocaust), oil barons, political isolationists, and some "establishment" German Jews. The "good guys" supported Israel; the "bad guys" opposed it. There was no cognitive dissonance between, or discomfort over, our liberal American values and our Jewish nationalistic aspirations. Electoral choices were easy for liberal Zionists: vote for liberal Democrats, like Adlai Stevenson, who supported Israel, and against Republicans like Dwight Eisenhower, who did not. In general, the center-left and the Democratic Party were more supportive of Israel than the center-right and the Republicans.

Although most *elected* Democratic political *leaders* currently reject overt anti-Israel programs, such as the Boycott, Divestment, and Sanctions movement ("BDS"), many Democratic *voters*, especially younger ones, support such programs. Many groups that identify with the Democratic Party—such as Move On, Code Pink, Occupy Wall Street, Black Lives Matter and intersectionalists[34]—reflect a strong anti-Israel bias, as do many student and faculty groups representing people

34 For a current definition of intersectionalism, see Wikipedia entry under "Intersectionality." https://en.wikipedia.org/wiki/Intersectionality

of color, feminists, and gay rights organizations that support the BDS and other anti-Israel initiatives. Some recently elected Democratic members of Congress, such as the so-called "Squad," are trying to move the Democratic Party away from support from Israel. And Bernie Sanders became the first major presidential candidate to express overtly anti-Israel views, to challenge the historic bi-partisan support for the Nation-State of the Jewish people, to hire for his staff virulently anti-Zionist and in some cases anti-Semitic extremists, and to praise bigots like Jeremy Corbyn and Ilhan Omar. Sanders's actions led other candidates to move closer to his views in an effort to appeal to younger, more radical Democrats who favor the Palestinians over Israel.

Today, support for Israel comes largely from older liberals, from young traditional Jews, and from conservatives, including many Evangelical Christians. Republican voters are more likely than Democratic voters to see Israel in a positive light.[35] Yet my generation of liberal Jews, and even the generations that follow mine, could not support a Republican Party or candidate because they reject so many of our deeply felt liberal values. We support racial, gender and sexual preference equality, a woman's right to choose abortion, gay marriage, gun control, the abolition of capital punishment, separation of church and state, health care for all, fair taxation, and reasonable immigration. We want a Supreme Court that is likely to favor these issues as well. We continue to support Israel, though many of us disagree with some of its policies, especially with regard to civilian settlements in the West Bank. Our disagreements about specific policies do not generally carry over to Israel's security needs and its right to defend its citizens against rocket attacks, terrorism, and threats from Hezbollah, Hamas, and Iran. We remain proudly pro-Israel and proudly liberal. But our

---

35 "[L]iberal Democrats have the lowest net sympathy for Israel." Saad (2019). "Americans, but not Liberal Democrats, Mostly Pro-Israel," The Gallup Organization. Retrieved from https://news.gallup.com/poll/247376/americans-not-liberal-democrats-mostly-pro-israel.aspx. The Pew Research Center found "While majorities in both parties have favorable views of the Israeli people, Republicans and Republican-leaning independents are more likely than Democrats and Democratic leaners to say this (77% vs. 57%)." (2019) https://www.people-press.org/2019/04/24/u-s-public-has-favorable-view-of-israels-people-but-is-less-positive-toward-its-government/.

numbers and influence within the left are shrinking. Liberal Zionists are becoming an endangered species.[36]

For supporters of Israel who are conservative on domestic issues, there is no conflict: they simply vote Republican, without having to compromise their principles or ideologies. For Democrats who don't support Israel but are liberal on domestic issues, there is also no conflict: simply vote Democrat, as a considerable number of Jews continue to do. But for liberal supporters of Israel who, like me, cannot support Republican domestic programs, there *is* a conflict: we support the Democratic *domestic* agenda, but not necessarily its foreign policies, especially, but not exclusively, with *regard to Israel*. As we will see, it's different in Great Britain, where the Conservative Party supports both Israel and much of the liberal social agenda.

The issue was put to me sharply in the 2012 presidential elections. I supported with enthusiasm President Obama's domestic policies and his Supreme Court appointments. But I was concerned about his policies with regard to Israel, and especially Iran. President Obama was certainly aware of this concern among a segment of his base, and so in the run-up to his 2012 re-election campaign, he invited me to the Oval Office, where he assured me of his strong support for Israel and his firm commitment to preventing Iran from obtaining nuclear weapons. I wanted to believe him, because I didn't want there to be any conflict between my domestic liberal values and my deep concern about Israel's security. So I credited what he told me and campaigned and voted for his re-election, despite some lingering reservations.[37]

The result of Obama's re-election was a continuation of positive domestic programs—health care, gay marriage, good judicial appointments—coupled with deeply disappointing policies regarding Israel, especially Iran. Obama also enraged many Jews, including me, by engineering a Security Council Resolution that falsely characterizes Israel's

36 There are disagreements, of course, over what constitutes "liberal" support for Israel. Does JStreet really "support" Israel, while opposing so many of its policies, actions and leaders? These issues are likely to come to the forefront during the 2020 election, as Joe Biden has enthusiastically accepted the endorsement of JStreet.

37 See Alan Dershowitz, "Obama's Legacy and the Iranian Bomb," *Wall Street Journal*, March 23, 2010.

"occupation" of the Western Wall, The Jewish Quarter, and the access roads to Hebrew University and Hadassah Hospital as a "flagrant violation of international law."[38] Jewish conservatives, who don't like or don't care about his domestic policies, said, "See, I told you so." Jewish hard-left opponents of Israel, who were pleased with Obama's policies, *both* with regard to domestic and Israel policies, also said, "See I told you so."

But liberal supporters of Israel were conflicted. We will continue to be conflicted as long as Democrats who support liberal domestic principles are less supportive of Israel than Republicans who support Israel but are less supportive of liberal domestic policies.

I was less conflicted during the 2016 election because Hillary Clinton, who won the nomination over Bernie Sanders, was seen as more supportive of Israel than either Obama or Sanders. We didn't know very much about Donald Trump's attitude toward Israel, but Clinton's pro-Israel views, coupled with her more liberal domestic policies and her experience and proven competence, made it easy for me and other liberal Zionists to vote for her, and she received the overwhelming support of Jewish liberals and Zionists. Had the Democrats nominated Bernie Sanders in 2016 to run against Donald Trump, the conflict for many liberal Jewish voters would have become most acute. The same is true of the 2020 election: Joe Biden's victory over Bernie Sanders will make it easier for liberal Jews to vote Democrat, despite President Trump's strong record on Israel. Some will, however, remain conflicted, because an increasing number of Democratic elected officials are moving away from support for Israel.

This conflict transcends Israel. There are many voters who strongly support the Democratic Party's domestic agenda, but are deeply suspicious about its foreign policy in general. The Obama administration created a vacuum by abandoning America's role as the leader of the free world and as an active supporter of democracies. While many of us were opposed to the American occupation of Iraq, we favor a more muscular foreign policy and a robust role for America in maintaining

38 See Alan Dershowitz, *Defending Israel* (New York: St. Martin's Publishing Group, 2019), p. 203.

liberal values around the world and in protecting the vital interests of America and its allies. We are not hawks, but nor are we doves. We are realists who understand that the projection of American power is essential to maintaining peace and promoting liberal values. President Obama may have been awarded the Nobel Peace Prize shortly after taking office, but in the view of many liberals, the world became a more dangerous and less free place during his tenure.

Many liberals were opposed to the Iran deal—I wrote a book entitled *The Case Against the Iran Deal*—but nor do we favor a military attack on Iran, except perhaps as an absolute last resort to prevent that regime from acquiring a nuclear arsenal. We do not sing "Bomb, Bomb Iran," as the late Senator John McCain did during his presidential campaign. We want to keep a strong military option on the table, but without actually deploying the Sword of Damocles unless absolutely necessary.[39] We are not neo-cons, because we do not buy into their economic domestic or hawkish foreign policies. Nor are we neo-libs, since we never abandoned our liberalism over the decades. But neither are we "paleo-libs," because we want our classic liberalism to be adaptive to current realities, rather than a return to some idyllic glory. We are a new incarnation of an old breed of domestic liberals and foreign policy realists who are now uncomfortable with elements of both parties, and with the extremist policies and attitudes of both the hard-right and left.

We haven't left the left. The left, especially the radical left, has left us. And many in the center-left, especially among the young, seem to be following the lead of their more radical fellow Democrats. Elements within both the Democratic and Republican parties have changed. Some Democrats are moving away from the traditional Democratic approach to foreign policy, especially but not exclusively with regard to the Middle East, and many Republicans have moved toward an approach to social issues that is based more on fundamentalist religious values than on libertarian or traditional conservative values. We are seeking a third way, but in the short term, we will probably have to

39 Alan Dershowitz, "Dershowitz: J Street Makes an Attack on Iran More Likely," *Newsmax*, August 16, 2012.

choose between the two existing imperfect alternatives, while seeking to pressure both parties to move closer to our centrist values.

Nor is the dissatisfaction with the left limited to foreign policy. It also includes the "identity politics" that elevates race, gender, ethnicity, sexual preference, and other particular characteristics over shared American values. This shift leads to the kind of double standard in both domestic and foreign policy that erodes principles of equality, civil liberties, and basic fairness. We reject the extremism of "Occupy Wall Street" and the parochialism of "Black Lives Matter." We recognize the realities of structural racism in the United States, but for us, all lives matter equally. We care deeply about the needless death of every black person, regardless of whether it is at the hands of a white policeman or a black gang member.

In some respects, but not in others, the dilemma liberals currently confront is a variation on an old conflict between centrist liberals and hard-left radicals. Genuine liberals—who believe in tolerance, freedom of expression, due process, and democratic values—have always been targeted by the radical left as traitors to "the cause." The Mensheviks were the enemies of the Bolsheviks; the Roosevelt liberals were the enemies of the 1930s Communists; the NAACP and Martin Luther King were the enemies of Malcolm X and The Black Panthers; and today's traditional liberals are the enemies of the newly minted radicals on the hard-left. We are not yet "woke" to the virtues of extremism. We remain mired in the politics of the past. We really are willing to compromise in order to get half-loaves. The "revolution," Alexandria Ocasio-Cortez warns us, is passing us by. She is wrong. It is not passing us by. We are not ignoring it. We are actively fighting against her "revolution" and in favor of changing some outcomes without tearing down existing institutions that have generally served us well.

This conflict between traditional liberalism and contemporary radicalism is being played out on a micro-level in universities around the world, and more recently on American campuses, including the Ivy League. Radical students are demanding restrictions on freedom of expression in the interest of "safe spaces," "political correctness," and protection against "micro-aggressions" and other forms of offensive speech. They insist that students and faculty members who disagree with their approach to racial, gender, and political issues—especially white, heterosexual males—be required to undergo "sensitivity training." When my grandson was an undergraduate at Harvard and a member of the *Lampoon*, the Harvard humor magazine, he attended the Harvard-Yale football game with a friend, who held up a humorous sign that read "Tackling is a micro-aggression." Some people laughed, but others berated them for their "insensitivity" toward minorities and accused them of a micro-aggression and of "politically incorrect behavior" that warranted discipline or training. "It's a joke," replied my grandson. "Well, it's not funny," insisted the political correctness "police."

These young radicals and their like-minded professors *know* the *truth* and they see no need to be exposed to uncomfortable *lies*, other perspectives, or humor. Their truths are absolute, while other truths are relative. And there is nothing funny about ideological purity. Many standup comedians now refuse to perform at colleges—as one put it: "My comedy is designed to offend everyone. That doesn't work on campuses." Liberals, on the other hand, understand that the quest for truth is a never-ending process, and that humor can be part of that process.

Ultimate truth, especially in the realm of politics, morality, law, or economics, is an illusory holy grail. It will never be found. Just as the struggle for liberty never stays won,[40] so too, the search for truth never ends. One truth begets others, with a great many falsehoods along the way. As the great Judge Learned Hand once put it: "The spirit of liberty is the spirit which is not too sure that it is right."[41] And that spirit must welcome conflicting views, even deeply offensive ones, into the open marketplace of ideas. The enemies of liberty reject that marketplace, just as they reject liberalism itself as class-based "privilege" that they want to see "checked." They have little tolerance for intellectual diversity, while demanding racial and other forms of diversity that bring to campus more students and faculty who share

---

40 Attributed to Roger Baldwin, the former head of the ACLU.

41 Judge Learned Hand, "The Spirit of Liberty," Central Park, New York. May 21, 1944.

their profiles, ideology, and often intolerance. They disdain Israel and other Western democracies, while refusing to criticize third-world tyrannies that reject equality based on gender and sexual preference. The "safe spaces" protections against "micro-aggressions" they demand for themselves and their allies, they deny to Jewish supporters of Israel, and Christians who seek to promote their faith on campus.

Anti-Israel zealots have tried to, and sometimes succeeded in, hijacking left-wing agendas involving race, gender, and economics, and demanding the inclusion of anti-Israel agenda items. They cite the sociological jargon of "intersectionality" to insist that you cannot be a true leftist on domestic issues without demonizing Israel for its oppression of Palestinians and America for its imperialism. They deliberately ignore the discrimination against Palestinians who live in Lebanon, Syria, and other mid-East countries.

Many radical feminists and gays refuse to condemn the sexism and homophobia of the enemies of Israel (and often America), while reserving their wrath for the imperfections of the Nation State of the Jewish People. This has led some traditional feminists and champions of gay rights, such as Phyllis Chesler, to accuse the left of abandoning its long-cherished values in favor of bigoted identity politics.[42] Perhaps the most absurd example of this phenomenon is the accusation by some gay and lesbian academics that Israel is guilty of "pinkwashing," that is, using its excellent record on gay rights to cover—or whitewash—its policies with regard to Palestinians. They invoke "intersectionality," championed by hard-left academics, to persuade allegedly oppressed groups to join together against the dominant power structure, even when some of the "oppressed" groups, such as radical Muslims, oppress other groups, such as gays and women. Jews, Zionists, Christians, and others are systematically excluded by radical left intersectionalists despite being oppressed in many parts of the world and on many campuses.

Some traditional liberals have gone so far as to stop supporting feminist, gay, and Afro-centric Black groups, because they don't want

---

42 John Sutherland, "The Ideas Interview: Phyllis Chesler," *The Guardian*, April 3, 2006.

to empower movements that seek to demonize and delegitimize Israel. While I continue to support such groups because I agree with their core mission of equality, I must admit that I sometimes do so with a sense of ambivalence and anger at their bigotry, selective outrage and hypocrisy toward the Nation State of the Jewish People.

This conflict between liberal and hard-left values, especially on campuses (where everything is exaggerated) augurs poorly for the future of traditional liberalism and suggests that the conflict about which I am writing will only get worse as the students of today become the leaders of tomorrow. I still hope that traditional liberal values will win out in the end, much like they did a generation earlier, when the radicalism embodied by Students for a Democratic Society gave way to the centrism of the Clinton Democrats. But as the hard-left's influence grows in the Democratic Party again, I worry that the party may be leaving me, and other centrist liberals, for good. They take our support for granted because they know we have nowhere to go. We cannot vote for a Republican Party dominated by right-wing extremists who reject basic liberal values.

The presidency of Donald Trump has created confusion among many liberal, pro-Israel voters. We approved of his recognition of Jerusalem as Israel's capital and of the Golan Heights as part of Israel (subject to subsequent negotiations), and of his tougher policy toward Iran's quest for a nuclear arsenal. But many of us disagreed with his decision to remove U.S. troops from Syria, thus exposing the Kurds to Turkish aggression. We are uncertain what he means when he says he wants to bring our troops home from the Mid-East. We don't like his policies, attitudes, and statements regarding immigration, but nor do we believe in open borders. We seek compromise solutions to complex issues such as immigration, health care, gun control, climate change, economic inequality, and homelessness.

Over the past several years, I have been making these observations in my speeches and public appearances. Invariably, dozens of people come up and say, "That's me! I, too, am a domestic liberal who supports Israel and a more muscular foreign policy, and I'm conflicted. I can't vote for Democrats who demonize Israel, or for Republicans who are anti-gay rights, women's rights, and other liberal programs. I like what President Trump has said and done on Israel, but not on other issues about which I care deeply. What should I do?"

Hence this book. It describes our conflict and proposes ways to address it. It also makes the case for a renewed and re-invigorated centrist liberalism that eschews the extremes of both left and right.

The terms "liberal" and "conservative" have taken on different meanings over time and place. These different meanings manifest themselves both in the context of American domestic politics, where "liberal" has become a "dirty word" with which both Republicans and radical Democrats seek to smear their political enemies, and in the context of American campuses, where hard-left radicals direct the word liberal with disdain against centrists who support traditional liberal values such as academic freedom, freedom of expression, and due process. Indeed, on many campuses, traditional liberals have allied themselves with traditional conservatives in seeking to combat attacks upon these eternal, if old-fashioned, values from both the extreme left and the fundamentalist right. We reject the notion that the values are anachronistic and unsuited to current times. We believe they are enduring and applicable to all times and places. We know from history that although today they are being denied to liberals and conservatives, in our past they were denied to radicals. "Civil liberties for me but not for thee" backfires over the long run.

Even within organizations such as the ACLU, Amnesty International, Human Rights Watch, and the NAACP, conflict has arisen between traditional liberals and civil libertarians, on the one hand, and radical elements that place more emphasis on what they see as progressive outcomes than on fair and open processes, on the other hand.

It is important to note that this is not simply a replay of previous episodes in our history, when former liberals left the left and joined the right—as many did in the 1930s, and then again in the 1960s and 1970s over Israel, urban crime, and affirmative action. Many of those erstwhile leftists had little difficulty embracing some right-wing domestic values, while challenging others. Indeed, they became *leaders* of the neo-con right, and commendably helped rid it of its anti-Semitic fringe, as represented by bigots such as Pat Buchanan and Joseph Sobran.

These neocons helped to redefine American conservatism, while accepting many of its domestic platform planks, such as judicial restraint, lower taxes on the wealthy, opposition to race-based affirmative action, a weakening of the wall of separation between church and state, reduced rights for those accused of crimes, and opposition to national health care. They also favored a more muscular foreign policy and increased American support for Israeli right-wing politicians.

Many among the current generation of liberals, like me, who feel abandoned by the left are unwilling to abandon their long-held liberal values. They want an activist Supreme Court, progressive taxation, effective affirmative action, a high wall of separation between church and state, the exclusionary rule and other protections for the accused, generous health care for all, and reasonable immigration policies. We want to remain liberals, and we want the Democratic Party to maintain its liberal values and to reject the illiberal demands of its hard-left wing, including, but not limited to, the abandonment of Israel and the subordination of freedom of expression and due process to mandated political correctness.

Many reasonable conservatives, especially those who come from liberal backgrounds, agree with some of these domestic goals, but they place more emphasis on their disagreements with Democrats over foreign policy issues. They are willing, therefore, to subordinate some of their domestic liberal values to what they regard as the greater good. Another complicating factor is that some (but certainly not all) of the older, traditional liberals have become wealthy enough to benefit from Republican economic policies. They may have a motive, whether conscious or unconscious, to vote Republican, but some are uncomfortable explicitly basing their votes on financial self-interests. ("If I am for myself alone, what am I?") We were brought up to believe that liberals do not vote their pocketbooks; conservatives do. Their disagreements over Democratic foreign policy provide a justification for voting for a party that also helps their bottom line, without requiring them to acknowledge their possible partial financial motive (what psychologists would call "secondary gain") for voting Republican.

Other former liberals honestly believe that conservative economic policies are better not only for them, but for the economy in general, and for working class people in particular. They point to the economic gains that were achieved for many under President Trump, before the Coronavirus. I have brilliant and compassionate friends who take that view and try to get me to agree. Thus far, I remain unconvinced, but with an open mind. I agree that this is an empirical issue about which reasonable people can, and do, disagree. I do not know which side is correct, though my own liberalism inclines me to resolve doubts in favor of liberal economic policies—such as higher taxes for the wealthy and higher minimum wages—that would immediately help level the playing field, but I acknowledge that those who disagree may turn out to be correct.

As is often the case, Israel may be the canary in the coal mine. It is the symptom of a larger, more pervasive problem. While the abandonment of Israel by the hard-left has precipitated the conflict that many liberals have in continuing to adhere to the left in general and to support the Democratic Party in particular, there are many issues transcending Israel that have contributed to this dilemma. These include foreign as well as domestic policy shifts by the Democratic Party brought about as a result of the demands by the hard-left. At the same time, shifts by the Republican Party in response to demands from the religious right have made the conflict more acute. Indeed, even when it comes to Israel, many on the religious right have gone well beyond what liberal supporters of Israel espouse. This includes continuing settlement activity on the West Bank, refusing any compromise over Jerusalem, and denying the right of the Palestinians to a non-militarized state. We were appalled by the Reverend Pat Robertson's suggestion that God had struck down Israel's Prime Ministers Rabin and Sharon for "dividing God's land."[43] Many of these views seem driven by radical interpretations of biblical scripture, old-fashioned bigotry, and racism directed towards Arabs and Muslims. Some are motivated by legitimate security concerns and an unwillingness to reward terrorism. There is no perfect solution for liberals who feel abandoned by

---

43 Sonja Barisic, "Pat Robertson Links Sharon's Stroke to God's Wrath." *The Seattle Times*, Jan. 5, 2006.

the hard-left but who cannot join the right because of its obeisance to religious and political zealots.

For some traditional liberal Democrats, the foreign policy issues outweigh the importance of the domestic issues. They support the right of a woman to choose, of gays to marry and the rest of the traditional liberal agenda, which would incline them to vote Democrat. But they regard the foreign policy issues, especially but not exclusively with respect to Israel, as more important and more likely to be influenced by who is president. My brother-in-law, Marvin Cohen, a brilliant psychologist who opposed the war in Vietnam and supports much of the domestic liberal agenda of the Democratic Party, decided to vote for Republican presidential candidates after 9/11. His reasoning is that the domestic rights he cares about have been made relatively secure by the Supreme Court and are unlikely to be affected by a Republican president, whereas the foreign and defense policy issues that he also cares about are very much dependent on who is in the Oval Office. He believes that the religious right has lost the battle over abortion and gay rights, just as the racist right lost the battle over civil rights in the 1960s. History is moving quickly against the kind of bigotry represented by these hard-right forces, particularly among the young who represent the future. He thinks that it is time to move beyond these divisive domestic issues and focus more on the current dangers we face from Jihadist Islam and other external enemies. For him, Fundamentalist Christians are not our enemies, even if we disagree with their efforts to Christianize America. Islamic Jihadists are our enemies, because they want to impose their religious beliefs by force and violence, rather than by proselytization and the ballot box. Their defeat must become our priority, and the Republicans are more deeply committed to fighting against these enemies.

While Marvin and I share many similar values, we disagree about how to calibrate their relative importance. I am not as sanguine about the endurance of our Supreme Court victories with regard to gender, sexual preference, race, and religion. I worry that a Republican Supreme Court could set us back considerably. I have come down differently on the weighing process and have continued to vote for Democratic candidates—at least for now. I will do everything in my power to try to influence Democratic candidates to support Israel, to continue to promote liberal values, and to resist the pressures of the illiberal hard-left wing of the party. My point in mentioning my brother-in-law is that reasonable people—especially those who are conflicted—can assess priorities differently and cast their votes accordingly. I respect the views of my brother-in-law and those who share his priorities. I refuse to demonize those with whom I reasonably disagree, unlike some of my former left-wing friends, who have demonized me for taking a different position on the constitutionality of efforts to impeach President Trump.

Nor will I demonize my friends who remain liberal Zionists but prioritize domestic issues over concerns regarding Israel. For these liberal mirror-images of my conservative brother-in-law, continuing to vote for the Democrats remains an easy choice. For those of us who prioritize domestic and foreign policy issues roughly equally, the choice is harder.

The goal of this book is to analyze how politically perplexed citizens—who are torn between liberal domestic values that incline them to support Democratic candidates and foreign policy and other values that might incline them to support Republican candidates—might think about this conflict. As a teacher for half a century, I never told my students what values to accept or which candidates to support. I always helped guide them to conclusions based on their own sets of values. I do the same in this book. I do not tell readers whether to support Democratic or Republican candidates. Instead, I try to sort out both the domestic and foreign policy values that each reader might possess, and set out a process for assessing these values and prioritizing them.

Each reader must think for her or himself about the comparative strength of each of their values and how they might prioritize them in an effort to come to rational conclusions regarding candidates and political parties. This book tries to be a guide rather than a piece of political advocacy for one party or another. Some readers will analyze their values and priorities in a manner that will make them vote for Democratic candidates, while others will be inclined to vote for Republicans. That is as it should be in a democracy.

This book is a defense of liberalism and its renewed relevance in our time. It makes the case for preferring classic liberal values and programs over radical-left and reactionary right-wing agendas. It makes the more general case for centrism over extremism—why our country has thrived because it has an enduringly strong centrist base, as contrasted with other countries that have a history of alternating left- and right-wing extremism. It also makes the case for dialogue about difference, instead of demonization and *ad hominem* attacks.

It seeks, by reason and empiricism, to restore contemporary liberalism to its important place in the American political landscape, and attempts to persuade centrists from both the left and right, who today eschew the liberal label in favor of calling themselves progressives or moderate conservatives, that they belong in the big tent of centrist liberalism. The case for centrist liberalism is powerful, and the need for it in a world of growing extremism is greater than ever. It is better than other "isms," as I will show in Chapter 5. In the next chapter, I explore the roots of liberalism in the enlightenment and in the writings of John Stuart Mill.

CHAPTER 3

The Theoretical Sources of Classic Liberalism—John Stuart Mill[44]

Liberalism, as a philosophy of governance, has deep roots in Europe, and especially Great Britain and France. Jefferson was influenced by John Locke, Montesquieu, Voltaire, and other enlightenment philosophers. But modern liberalism owes its greatest debt to the utilitarian philosophies of Jeremy Bentham and John Stuart Mill, especially Mill.

Few ideas regarding classic liberalism have had so profound an intellectual influence within Western democracies as John Stuart Mill's "one very simple principle." The principle, governing the proper allocation of state power and individual liberty, was articulated by Mill in his 1859 essay entitled "On Liberty." In Mill's words:

> That principle is, that the sole end for which mankind are warranted, individually or collectively, in interfering with the liberty of action of any of their number, is self-protection. That the only purpose for which power can be rightfully exercised over any member of a civilized community, against his will, is to prevent harm to others. His own good, either physical or moral, is not a sufficient warrant. He cannot rightfully be compelled to do or forbear because it will be

44 This chapter is adapted from an introduction I wrote for John Stuart Mill's *On Liberty and Utilitarianism* (New York: Bantam, 1993).

> better for him to do so, because it will make him happier, because, in the opinion of others, to do so would be wise, or even right. These are good reasons for remonstrating with him, or reasoning with him, or persuading him, or entreating him, but not for compelling him, or visiting him with any evil in case he do otherwise. To justify that, the conduct from which it is desired to deter him, must be calculated to produce evil to some one else. The only part of the conduct of any one, for which he is amenable to society, is that which concerns others. In the part, which merely concerns himself, his independence is, of right, absolute. Over himself, over his own body and mind, the individual is sovereign.[45]

Like other profoundly influential principles, such as the Bible's "Thou shalt love thy neighbor like thyself" and Kant's "So act, that the rule on which thou actest would admit of being adopted as a law by all rational beings," Mill's principle is as simple as it is eloquent (at least in conception—Mill was the first to acknowledge its difficulties in application). The power of the state may not be used to compel a reasoning adult to do or not do anything solely because such action or inaction would be better for the adult.

At its core, Mill's approach to compulsion, though directed at the state, challenged the approach underlying most traditional religions, which employ compulsion, often assisted by the state, to make

---

45 Mill made it clear that his principles applied only to "human beings in the maturity of their faculties" and granted to the State the power to determine, within reason, the age of "manhood and womanhood." The explicit inclusion of womanhood reflected more than syntactical completeness; Mill wrote eloquently in favor of women's equality in the home, at the ballot box, and in the world at large.

John Stuart Mill, *The Subjection of Women* (Philadelphia: Lippincott, 1869).

While support for women's rights was uncharacteristic of his circle during the mid-nineteenth century, Mill's implicit acceptance of colonialism was all too typical. He exempted from his principle "those backward states of society in which the race itself may be considered as in its nonage." For such "barbarians," Mill paternalistically concluded, benevolent "despotism is a legitimate form of government," since liberty has no application "to any state of things anterior to the time when mankind may have become capable of being improved by free and equal discussion."

But neither his progressive inclusion of women nor his regressive exclusion of "backward" people is central to Mill's principle and its remarkable influence on Western society.

adherents take actions that are deemed morally or religiously beneficial only to them.

It is interesting that this principle was, for Mill, based entirely on utilitarian considerations, such as those articulated by Bentham: "It is proper to state that I forgo any advantage which could be derived to my argument from the idea of abstract right [since] I regard utility as the ultimate appeal on all ethical questions." There are, however, persuasive utilitarian arguments in favor of compelling adults to do certain things that would make them happier and better people. Indeed, if a truly benevolent despot really knew the secret of maximizing happiness for everyone, there would surely be many utilitarians who would feel compelled to grant him the power to do what no democracy has thus far succeeded in doing: namely, producing a universally happy society.

In the end, however, Mill is not at his best in attempting to justify his principle solely on conventional utilitarian grounds. Though Mill himself eschews all advantage to his argument from "abstract right," that does not necessarily mean that those who reject utilitarianism and accept abstract rights must reject Mill's principle. Even as an abstract right or as part of a rights-based system, Mill's principle has much to commend it. This is an instance where the power of the principle transcends the strength of the underlying justification offered by its proponent. I think it is true today that a considerable number of non-utilitarians do, in fact, accept Mill's basic principle with as few or as many variations as orthodox utilitarians who accept it.

Indeed, it is fair to say that the fundamentals of Mill's principles have become almost a conventional wisdom of Western society, at least among its intellectuals both on the center left and center right. It is generally taken for granted as a premise of debate concerning the proper allocation of state power and individual freedom. To be sure, there are some state paternalists, especially among the religious right, and the socialist left, who still believe that it is the proper function of government to compel adults to do what is deemed best for them. But the vast majority of contemporary Western thinkers—whatever their philosophical bent—seem to accept the basic Millian principle that it is not the proper function of government to compel conduct solely in order to improve the life of an adult who does not necessarily want his or her life so improved by government compulsion.

Many philosophers reject the rigidity with which Mill stated his thesis. Others have greater difficulty than even he had in clearly distinguishing between actions that affect only the actor and those that have a discernible impact on others. But it is not easy to find many who categorically reject the core concept central to Mill's principle and who would grant the state the power to make reasoning adults take nontrivial actions that they have knowingly chosen not to take but that the state believes they should take in order to better themselves or make them happier. This is especially true in a nation as diverse and heterogeneous as the United States, where it would be difficult to reach a consensus on what constitutes the kind of betterment of happiness that could properly be imposed. As George Bernard Shaw put it: "Do not do unto others as you expect they should do unto you—their tastes may not be the same." But even in more homogenous democratic nations, Mill's core principle has become the conventional wisdom, at least in theory.

The best evidence of how influential Mill's principle has become—indeed, how it is presumed by most thinkers—may be the repeated efforts of those who would compel a given action against protesting individuals to rationalize such force by reference to the rights of others rather than by reference to the good of the compelled individual. Examples abound, but one will suffice to make the general point. A distinguished colleague of mine would seek to justify mandatory seat belt laws by rejecting the argument that "only the belt-wearer's own welfare [is] at risk." He argues instead that we should recognize that refusing to buckle up endangers:

> those who end up being injured or even killed in avoidable collisions when unbuckled drivers lose control of their cars. Quite simply, the seat-belt law prevents people from becoming loose objects when a car skids or veers into a tree or another vehicle; a belted driver is less likely to become a helpless spectator as his car is turned into an un-

> guided missile. Surely that is a legitimate exercise of society's power to protect the innocent, not the entering wedge of tyranny.[46]

While these observations may all have some small validity, they miss the big picture, namely, that seat belt laws have as their primary object the mandatory protection of the adult belt wearer. I, too, favor mandatory seat belt laws, but I recognize that support for such paternalistic legislation requires a compromise with Mill's principle. And it is a compromise I am prepared to make explicitly rather than uncomfortably try to squeeze seat belt laws into Mill's principle by invoking flying people and leaping logic.

My compromise would establish two significant exceptions to Mill's principle. The first I call the "light pinky of the law" exception. The second I call the "Thanks, I needed that" exception.

The "light pinky of the law" is at the opposite end of the continuum from the "heavy thumb of the law." It refers to regulations carrying minor financial penalties that are calculated to influence the behavior of people who really have no ideological objection to doing something that will help them but who don't care enough to take the step without some gentle nudging from the law. Seat belt laws are a perfect example. Most Americans will wear seat belts if the law requires them to and will not wear them if the law does not require them to. That may seem silly to any believer in rational, cost-benefit analysis. Why, after all, should a fifty-dollar fine work when the compelling statistical and clinical evidence that safety belts save lives does not work? The answer lies in the indisputable fact that most people do not rationally calculate the costs and benefits of their actions, particularly when the benefit is hypothetical, long-term, and statistically quite unlikely to come about. That is so even if the cost is as trivial as buckling up.

For a variety of reasons, the law often works where rational calculation does not. People do not generally want to be perceived—by themselves or others—as lawbreakers, even when the penalty is quite trivial. The law does have some kind of moral imperative that moves people

46 Lawrence Tribe, "The Seat-Belt Law Does Not Intrude on Freedom," *Boston Globe*, March 22, 1986, p. 11.

to action and inaction more powerfully than the mere economic cost attached to violation. To be sure, if the law is overused, or is used immorally or foolishly, much of that moral imperative may be diluted. But as of now, for most citizens of Western democracies, the law does work, at least in situations where it is used to nudge people into doing something relatively cost-free that promises some potential benefit.

That is why I, as a liberal, favor mandatory seat belt laws and other simple self-helping safety rules that are enforced with no more than small fines. But the "light pinky of the law" exception to Mill's principle should not, in my view, be expanded beyond the narrow areas in which it is appropriate. To make my point, I will argue that mandatory motorcycle helmet laws—though similar in many respects to seat belt laws—may exceed the narrow bounds of my exception. The distinction may be subtle, but it is real: Most car drivers who would not wear seat belts if the law were silent are not conscientiously opposed either to seat belts or to the legal requirement that they be worn; they are simply lazy, forgetful, or unconcerned; they will do whatever the law nudges them to do. Most motorcycle riders who would not wear helmets in the absence of a law seem to be conscientiously opposed both to helmets and to the legal requirement that they wear them. If I am right about the difference, then mandatory helmet laws are really different from mandatory seat belt laws—at least for those cyclists who care deeply about their freedom to maim and kill themselves. For the conscientiously opposed cyclist—as distinguished from the car driver who couldn't care less whether he buckles up or doesn't—the legal requirement that he wear a helmet will be perceived as a fundamental denial of freedom rather than as a trivial nudge from the state. He will feel the heavy thumb of the law upon him, rather than the light pinky that will be felt by the typical car driver. who would not buckle up if he did not "have to."

But what about those few car drivers who feel as strongly about seat belt laws as the helmet-free cycle fanatics feel about the helmet laws? There are two ways of dealing with this minority: If we lived in a totally honest society where all defendants always told the truth about why they violated the law, there could be an exception written into the seat belt law for conscientious objectors who could show that they had thought through the issue and had come to an ideological position against buckling up (or against being compelled to buckle up). But because many people who were caught unbuckled would falsely claim that they were conscientious objectors when they were merely lazy, the exception might swallow up the rule. The other way of dealing with the small number of conscientious objectors is simply to regard the fifty-dollar fine as a tax or an insurance surcharge for engaging in behavior that is dangerous to themselves but for which society in general will have to pay. In other words, society would be telling these people that they are not forbidden from driving unbuckled; they must simply pay a small price for doing so.[47]

In no case, under the "light pinky of the law" exception, would I ever put a dissenter in prison—or punish him or her harshly—for refusing to take an action that would benefit only him or her. I would reserve serious penalties for those who squarely fit within Mill's principle.

This brings us to the second exception, which, in my view, sometimes justifies mandatory seat belt laws designed to prevent injuries to those who would not otherwise buckle up, as well as some other limited state compulsion designed to help only the compelled individual. The "Thanks, I needed that" exception derives from the typical scene in old grade-B movies in which one character is out of control and the other character slaps him in the face to restore his control. The slapped character invariably says, "Thanks, I needed that," thus demonstrating his after-the-fact appreciation of his friend's paternalistic assault. Even Mill would permit state compulsion to prevent the mentally ill—those not capable of rational thought—from harming themselves. But my exception would, perhaps, go a bit further. I would justify state compulsion to prevent—at least temporarily—a distraught but rational adult from killing (or otherwise inflicting irreversible serious harm on) himself or herself. I would regard it as morally permissible—indeed, perhaps morally imperative—to try to prevent such self-inflicted harm if I can do so without unreasonable risk to myself or others. I would do so in the expectation that after the person calmed down and thought it through, he would thank me—perhaps not literally, but at least in his

---

47 See Mill, *On Liberty* pp. 24-26.

own mind. If I were wrong in a particular case, I would still not regret what I had done, because the person has an eternity to be dead, and I would not regard myself as having denied him much if I deprived him of several additional hours or even days of death. If, on the other hand, I were to err on the side of not preventing the suicide of a person who would indeed have thanked me for doing so, then I would have contributed to denying him the rest of his life.

As with the motorcycle helmet example, I would not apply the thank-you exception to rational adults who have carefully thought through the issue of suicide over a substantial period of time and have decided to end their lives.

It is somewhat more questionable whether seat belt laws fit comfortably within the thank-you exception as well. The vast majority of car drivers who grumble over buckling up would certainly say thank you if they were involved in an accident in which their lives (or limbs) were saved by wearing the seat belt they would not have worn but for the law. But would they say thank you after each car trip during which they were required to buckle up, or only when—and if—they were involved in an accident?

There is a considerable danger in expanding the thank-you exception to the point where it could swallow up much of Mill's principle. A large number of hypothetical paternalistic compulsions—for example, those directed against smoking, overeating, consuming too much sugar, or not exercising—could be justified by reference to a mirror-image version of the thank-you exception. I can easily imagine angry people on their deathbeds complaining about the lack of compulsion that allowed them to smoke, eat, and couch potato themselves to death. "Why didn't you make me stop smoking? I would be thanking you today if you had!" Well, one response to that hypothetical conversation is: "No, you wouldn't be thanking me if you were up and around and healthy, because you wouldn't appreciate—as you now do—the importance of not smoking. It required you to come face-to-face with death for you to understand why you should not have smoked, and now it is too late." The more persuasive answer is that there is a crucial difference between a brief one-shot act of compulsion, such as preventing the distraught person from jumping out the window or taking poison, and a long-term, lifestyle-changing compulsion, such as that required to make a person stop smoking, overeating, or not exercising. The state should be far more reticent about enforcing long-term, lifestyle-changing compulsions on unwilling adults than it should be to risk not being thanked for a brief one-shot interference with an adult's liberty that may well be appreciated in retrospect.

I offer these two limited exceptions to Mill's principle to suggest that it is far better to argue about the limits of the principle itself than to accept it as an almost biblical (or constitutional) rule of action and then try to find ways to squeeze what are really exceptions into the parameters of the principle.

We live today in a far more interdependent society than the one in which Mill lived. Even in Mill's time and before, there were those who believed that "no man is an island, entire of itself."[48] Mill recognized, of course, that actions that cause harm to the actor often create ripples that touch others.[49] As we shall see later, however, Mill is not at his best in dealing with such matters of degree. Nor is it clear how Mill would have applied his principle to somewhat more complex and multifaceted problems than those he discussed.

Consider, for example, some current controversies on which Mill's principle may bear differently in today's America than it appeared to bear in Mill's England. Mill may or may not have known that smoking harms the lungs and heart of the smoker. But even had he known that fact, he would still not countenance legislation banning smoking. He might, perhaps, have approved of labeling laws designed to give the smoker information necessary to decide whether the present pleasure of the puff was worth the possible pain of the future. Today, we know that smoking hurts not only the lungs and hearts of smokers, but also the health of nonsmokers. That might well have led Mill to conclude that adults have the right to inhale but not to exhale—at least not in the presence of non-consenting adults or children. Just as your right to

48 John Donne, "Meditation XVII," in *The Norton Anthology of English Literature*, vol. I (New York: M.H. Abrams, 1979), p. 1108.

49 See Mill, *On Liberty*, pp. 24-25.

swing your fist ends at the tip of my nose, so, too, your right to puff on a cigarette ends at the edge of my nostrils.

In Mill's day—indeed, until quite recently—pornography and obscenity where regarded as "moral" issues akin to masturbation. Both were thought to be bad for the soul, the psyche, and the sexuality of the viewer or reader. As such, Mill would find no basis for preventing adults from indulging in smut in the privacy of their bedrooms. Now, however, we are told by some feminists that those who view or read pornography will be more likely to engage in violent actions against non-consenting women. This is not the place to rehash the empirical debate over whether pornography causes rape or other violence toward women. The issue here is a normative one: if it could be shown that pornography did cause harm, not only to its consumers, but also to others who do not consent to its availability, may the state properly prevent its consumption, even in private?[50]

A similar controversy, but with an interesting twist, surrounds the state regulation of addictive drugs, especially heroin. By criminalizing heroin—a chemical that harms the user but does not itself make him or her more prone to violence—the state increases the cost of obtaining the highly addictive drug. The "market" cost of heroin would be quite low if it were available by medical prescription, but because it is illegal, its cost is many times higher. This increased cost causes most heroin addicts to commit many more acquisitive and predatory crimes against innocent people then they might otherwise commit (I say "otherwise," because many heroin addicts have criminal histories). Accordingly, the criminalization of heroin violates Mill's principle in two ways: first, it employs the power of society to compel (or at least try to compel) the adult user to forbear from doing something because not doing it would be better for him or her; second, by doing so, it causes harm to others.

This may sound like a simplistic analysis, since the causes of crime and the effects of addiction are so complex and varied. Moreover, this analysis is not as clearly applicable to other drugs, such as crack cocaine, which may themselves make the user more prone to violence.

50 Mill addressed "offenses against decency" (ibid., pp. 108-9), but he contented himself with the conventional distinction between indecent acts done in public and in private.

But the heroin example makes an important point about the misuses of the criminal sanction.

Mill spoke indirectly to this issue in the context of prostitution and gambling. He concluded that "fornication" and "gambling" must be tolerated, but then he asked whether a person should "be free to be a pimp, or to keep a gambling-house?" He would probably have come to the same conclusion and asked the same question about the drug user (at least those who retain the power of rational thought) and the drug seller. Mill regarded the question of such professional accessories as "one of these which lie on the exact boundary line." It was clear to him, as it remains clear today to many liberals–though not to all liberal feminists–that the case for criminalizing the professional purveyor of vice is arguably stronger than the case for criminalizing the occasional consumer of vice.[51]

Another controversial set of contemporary issues also demonstrates the limitations on Mill's principle. The whole era of "fetal" rights is not really amenable to solution by reference to Mill's principle, because the essential dispute is over a question that Mill did not address: namely, is the fetus a part of the carrying woman and thus beyond the ken of compulsory state regulation? Or is the fetus a "someone else" that the state has the legitimate power to protect against abortion, abuse, or neglect?

Some argue, as the courts have sometimes implied, that the fetus becomes a "someone else" at the moment of viability–that is, when it would be capable of independent life outside the womb. Others argue that the fetus becomes a "someone else" when the pregnant woman makes the decision to carry to term rather than to abort. Under this latter approach, the state might have the power to compel a pregnant woman who had decided not to abort to refrain from excessive

---

51 Some feminists argue that the consumer creates the demand and is thus responsible for the ensuing harm to others. Many feminists demand that johns—occasional consumers of sex for hire—must be prosecuted if prostitutes are prosecuted. Some argue that *only* johns and pimps, but not prostitutes should be prosecuted. For a civil liberties perspective, see Alan M. Dershowitz, *Taking Liberties* (Chicago: Contemporary Books, 1988) pp. 90-91.

drinking or other activities that pose significant health risks to the "someone else" she has decided to carry to term.

In the last analysis, Mill's principle does not help us decide whether or when a fetus becomes a "someone else" –that is for theologians, biologists, judges, or perhaps each pregnant woman to decide. But Mill's rule can help us sort through some complex philosophical issues regarding the relationships between carrying woman and fetus–once it is decided that the fetus has become "someone else" deserving of some degree of state protection. A wise state may, of course, decline to exercise power–particularly the power of criminal law–in certain areas where it may well have legitimate authority to act. The relationship between woman and fetus may be such an area.[52]

One more general issue of complexity, alluded to earlier, may warrant brief further discussion. We live in an age in which people have become far more economically interdependent because of insurance, welfare, taxation, and other mechanisms for sharing the risks and costs of individual hardships. Thus, if some drivers buckle up and others do not, and if the cost of insurance or medical care will rise for all as the result of avoidable injuries caused by a driver's decision not to buckle up, then it can be argued that we all have a stake in every driver's buckling up. That argument can be taken, however, to absurd extremes. We non-skiers, non-bungee jumper, and non-hang gliders also have a stake in preventing daredevils from taking what we regard as undue risks to their limbs and our pocketbooks. We exercising, cholesterol-watching, fat-avoiding, one-drink-a day consumers have a stake in every greasy hamburger and kielbasa eaten by a couch potato whose clogged arteries will cost us money. Where would a reasonable line be drawn between compelling everyone to live a safe, healthy, moderate life, and permitting undue risk-takers to have their destructive lifestyle (and death wishes) subsidized by the rest of us?

One way of dealing with this issue is to impose risk costs on certain clearly dangerous activities. We already do that through differential

---

52 Mill put it this way: "As soon as any part of a person's conduct affects prejudicially the interest of others, society has jurisdiction over it, and the question whether the general welfare will or will not be promoted by interfering with it, becomes open to discussion." Mill, *On Liberty*, pp. 83-84.

insurance premiums based on risk factors such as smoking and hang gliding. It would not be unreasonable, in governments that make the wearing of seat belts optional, for insurance companies to give drivers who agree to buckle up a discount on the premium. Indeed, the state might even go further, in my view, and impose a tax on those who refuse to wear seat belts or motorcycle helmets. There already are special taxes in many states on cigarettes, the proceeds from which are used to reduce the societal costs attributable to smoking. I doubt that Mill would have had difficulty with a system that imposed the costs of risk taking more directly on the risk takers, so long as the risk taker remained free of state compulsion and could decide for him or herself whether to incur the risk and the cost.[53]

Mill recognized, of course, the interdependent nature even of his society. Paraphrasing John Donne, Mill wrote:

> No person is an entirely isolated being; it is impossible for a person to do anything seriously or permanently hurtful to himself, without mischief reaching at least to his near connexions, and often far beyond them. If he injures his property, he does harm to those who directly or indirectly derived support from it, and usually diminishes, by a greater or lesser amount, the general resources of the community. If he deteriorates his bodily or mental faculties, he not only brings evil upon all who depended on him for any portion of their happiness, but disqualifies himself for rendering the services which he owes to his fellow creatures generally; perhaps becomes a burthen on their affection or benevolence; and if such conduct were very frequent, hardly any offense that is committed would detract more from the general sum of good. Finally, if by his vices or follies a person does no direct harm to others, he is nevertheless (it maybe said) injurious by his example, and ought to be compelled to control

53 Some thinkers have suggested that individuals be allowed to opt out of all social welfare systems by agreeing not to use them even if they were desperate. But would the rest of us really be willing to see an opt-outer suffer without helping him or her? And would a system permitting such opting out be cost-efficient? These questions are beyond the scope of this chapter.

> himself, for the sake of those whom the sight or knowledge of his conduct might corrupt or mislead.

Having recognized this interdependence, Mill proceeded to reject it on the following grounds:

> But with regard to the merely contingent, or, as it may be called, constructive injury which a person causes to society, by conduct which neither violates any specific duty to the public, nor occasions perceptible hurt to any assignable individual except himself; the inconvenience is one which society can afford to bear, for the sake of the greater good of human freedom. If grown persons are to be punished for not taking proper care of themselves, I would rather it were for their own sake, than under pretense of preventing them from impairing their capacity of rendering to society benefits which society does not pretend it has a right to exact.

In the end, Mill merely gives us his preference: "the greater good of human freedom" over what he calls "the inconvenience" of "constructive injury" caused by the exercise of that freedom. It is a preference shared by most liberals, libertarians, and individualists, but not one shared by all communitarians or even utilitarians. This conflict has divided and will continue to divide people of goodwill who care about both freedom and responsibility.

There is one area of individual freedom that is not neatly amenable to Mill's general principle. That is the area of "liberty of thought and discussion." Mill makes some of the most powerful arguments for a liberal approach to freedom of speech that have ever been expressed by liberal writers. These arguments include historical, empirical, and logical arguments both in favor of the virtues of free expression and against the vices of censorship.

In his ringing defense of free speech, Mill rejects one of the bedrock arguments of American jurisprudence, namely, that "the marketplace of ideas" will inevitably produce truth:

> The dictum that truth always triumphs over persecution, is one of those pleasant falsehoods which men repeat after one another till they pass into commonplaces, but which all experience refutes. History teems with instances of truth put down by persecution.

He offers this observation in refutation of the theory, also rejected by American jurisprudence, that "truth may justifiably be persecuted because persecution cannot possibly do it any harm." Persecution can, in fact, destroy truths, not only in the short run but forever. How many truths must have perished forever in the Holocaust? How many with enslavement? How many with the genocide against native peoples in America and elsewhere? How many with the Inquisition, by the Stalinist purges, and on the Cambodian killing fields? Truth is not a piece of matter or a unit of energy that will survive pummeling and emerge unscathed in one form or another at one time or another. It is a fragile and ethereal aspiration, easily buried, difficult to retrieve, and capable of being lost forever. That is why every time an idea is censored, a person with an idea killed, or a culture destroyed, we risk irredeemable injury to the corpus of human knowledge. And that is why it is always better to err on the side of more speech, more expression, more advocacy—even when the benefits seem distant and the costs immediate. American jurisprudence and Mill's philosophy reach the same conclusion about the benefits of unfettered exchange, though by somewhat different routes.

Mill argued persuasively even for the freedom to err—the right to be wrong. He offered a utilitarian justification for the encouraging of false arguments against the received wisdom, because "teachers and learners go to sleep at their post, as soon as there is no enemy in the field."

One of Mill's most compelling arguments has particular applications to the debate over "speech codes," "safe spaces," and "political correctness" on contemporary college and university campuses. Mill understood more than a century ago what many proponents of speech codes seem to ignore today: namely, that censorship is almost never content-neutral. Codes that purport to ban "offensive" or "intemperate" words are inevitably invoked selectively against politically incorrect offensive or intemperate words. Censorship is a weapon wielded by those in power against those who are not. On college and university campuses, those in power—or those who can influence those in power—may be very different from those in power in the outside world, but Mill's point remains persuasive:

> With regard to what is commonly meant by intemperate discussion, namely invective, sarcasm, personality, and the like the denunciation of these weapons would deserve more sympathy if it were ever proposed to interdict them equally to both sides; but it is only desired to restrain the employment of them against the prevailing opinion: against the un-prevailing they may not only be used without general disapproval, but will be likely to obtain for him who uses them the praise of honest zeal and righteous indignation.

Mill would argue, of course, that even if we could create what I have called "a symmetrical circle of civility" or "ism-equity"—namely, the identical rules of discourse for all, regardless of the content of their views—it would still be wrong to restrict speech based on factors such as offensiveness, incivility, or rudeness.

The hard question for Mill—indeed, for any utilitarian advocate of free speech—is what should happen when freedom of speech clashes directly with Mill's principle authorizing state compulsion "to prevent harm to others." Here Mill is his sloppiest as a thinker:

> No one pretends that actions should be as free as opinions. On the contrary, even opinions lose their immunity, when the circumstances in which they are expressed are such as to constitute their expression a positive instigation to some mischievous act. An opinion that corn-dealers are starvers of the poor, or that private property is robbery, ought to be unmolested when simply circulated through the press, but may justly incur punishment when delivered orally to an excited mob assembled before the house of corn-dealer, or when handed about among the same mob in the form of a placard. Acts, of whatever kind, which, without justifiable cause, do harm to others, may be, and in the more important cases absolutely require to be, controlled by the unfavorable sentiments, and, when needful, by the active interference

> of mankind. The liberty of the individual must be thus far limited; he must not make himself a nuisance to other people.

Mill's last sentence—that a speaker may not "make himself a nuisance to other people"—contains the seeds of a system of pervasive state censorship. Mill probably intended the concept *nuisance* to be construed in the narrowest possible way—say, by reference to his prior example of inciting an excited mob. But it is surely capable of being applied to almost any manner of offensive speech, ranging from religious proselytization to pornography. It has given rise to the deeply misunderstood and misapplied cliché, coined by Justice Holmes, that "falsely shouting fire in a theater" is not protected speech. Of course shouting "fire" is not *protected* speech: it isn't speech *at all*; it is the equivalent of falsely setting off a fire alarm. It is not intended to stimulate thinking. It does not communicate ideas. Shouting fire is an alarm *sound*, calculated to spur immediate action. Mill would have understood this better than did Holmes or others who promiscuously invoked the cliché to suppress speech.[54]

Mill's sketchy utilitarian argument for censorship is, in my view, shortsighted. A larger view would prefer—as the First Amendment to the United States Constitution prefers, and as Mill himself seems to prefer elsewhere—the benefits of relatively unabridged speech over the "inconvenience" of tolerating nuisances, even deeply offensive nuisances. Justice Louis Brandeis—another paragon of liberalism[55]—provided wiser counsel than Mill when he argued, in a case involving socialists who trespassed on private property as part of a protest against capitalism, that a free and open society should tolerate a certain degree of nuisance as a price worth paying for free and untrammeled expression.[56] We should have different rules for regulating non-expressive

---

54 For a criterion of Holmes's cliché, see Dershowitz, *Shouting Fire* pp. 141-147.

55 Brandeis was not always liberal in his decisions. He joined Justice Holmes's decision empowering the state to sterilize mentally incompetent women on eugenic grounds.

56 This is how Brandeis put it:

> But it is hardly conceivable that this court would hold constitutional a statute which punished as a felony the mere voluntary assembly with a society formed to teach that pedestrians have the moral right to cross an unenclosed, un-posted, waste lands and to advocate their doing so, even if there was an imminent danger that advocacy would lead to a trespass. The fact that speech is likely to

actions that pose a danger to others, and for censoring expressive speech that poses comparable dangers.[57] A single utilitarian calculus simply will not do in a society that values freedom of expression more highly than freedom of action. Our society is committed to the proposition that freedom of expression is the best guarantor of freedom of action. Our First Amendment expresses a far different calculus for regulating speech than for regulating non-expressive conduct, and that is as it should be. Your right to swing your fist should end at the tip of my nose, but your right to express your ideas should not necessarily end at the lobes of my ears.

In a letter written sixty years before *On Liberty*, Thomas Jefferson rejected the view that the "utterance of an opinion is an overt act, and if evidently immoral may be punished by law." He argued that "we have nothing to fear from the demoralizing reasoning of some, if others are left free to demonstrate their errors" and if "the law stands ready to punish the first criminal act produced by false reasoning. . . ." Though it is unclear whether Mill was directly influenced by Jefferson, it is clear that they were both influenced by earlier Enlightenment thinkers.[58]

In the end, John Stuart Mill's enduring contribution to the theory of liberalism is a remarkable tour de force. Flawed as it is in its applications, it provides no road map for liberalism because there can be no road map capable of taking us through the ever-shifting terrain of human civilization. But it is an important compass and guide to liberalism that points us in the proper direction as surely today as it did a century and a half ago. Every liberal (and centrist conservative)

> result in some violence or in destruction of property is not enough to justify its suppression. There must be the probability of serious injury to the State. Among free men, the deterrents ordinarily to be applied to prevent crime are education and punishment for violation of the law, not abridgement of the rights of free speech and assembly.
>
> *Whitney v. California*, 274 U.S. 357 (1927) (Justice Brandeis, concerning).

57 Distinguishing between action and speech will not always be easy, as demonstrated by the trespass case and others–such as the Boston Tea Party, flag burning, and cross burning. But the distinction, even if not subject to a bright line, is essential to any society, like ours, committed to elevating freedom of expression over freedom of action.

58 Alan Dershowitz, *Finding Jefferson* (Wiley, 2008), p. 197.

should look to Mill for inspiration and education. Every citizen of the world who aspires to freedom should reread Mill's *On Liberty* periodically and should consistently evaluate and challenge the actions of the state by reference to its simple but profound principle. Liberalism, in theory as well as practice, owes an enormous debt to enlightenment philosophers, and especially to John Stuart Mill. But we must not rest on Mill's laurels. We must adapt our liberal arguments to new realities, because as I will show in the coming chapter, rights come from experiences, and as experiences change, so must the justifications for maintaining and broadening our rights.

CHAPTER 4

A Liberal Perspective on the Source of Our Rights[59]

For liberals, rights play a central role in governance. Power without rights is tyranny. Liberals must therefore address the question: What is the source of our rights? Is it only existing laws that are subject to repeal? Do they come from "nature?" From "God?" If so, whose interpretation of nature? Whose God?

Our founding document of liberty, the Declaration of Independence, pointed to God as the source of our rights.[60] Among the "truths" that were regarded by our Founding Fathers as "self-evident" was the proposition that certain rights were "unalienable" because their source was neither government nor popular acceptance, but the endowment of the "Creator." What God gives, no human can take away. As the young Alexander Hamilton insisted on the eve of the American Revolution:

> The sacred rights of mankind are not to be rummaged for among old parchments or musty records . . . . They are written, as with a

59 Portions of this chapter are adapted from my book *Rights from Wrongs*.

60 *See* Chapter 6 *infra.*

> sunbeam, in the whole *volume* of human nature by the hand of the divinity itself and can never be erased or obscured by mortal power.[61]

Nor is this an anachronistic view. President George W. Bush put it this way in 2002: "We need common-sense judges who understand our rights were derived from God.[62] President Trump has echoed that point: "Our rights come from God Almighty, and they can never be taken away."

If only it were that simple! If only it were true that a God, in whom everyone believed, had come down from the heavens and given the entire world an unambiguous list of the rights with which He endowed us. How much easier it would be to defend the sacred rights from alienation by mere mortals, including presidents and legislators. Alas, the claim that rights were written down by the hand of the divinity is one of those founding myths to which we desperately cling, along with the giving of the Tablets to Moses on Sinai, the dictation of the Koran to Muhammad, and the discovery of the Gold Plates by Joseph Smith.

To the extent the divine source and inalienability of our rights are purported to be factual, history has proved our Founding Fathers plainly wrong: Every right has, in fact, been alienated by governments since the beginning of time. Within a generation of the establishment of our nation, the Founding Fathers rescinded virtually every right they previously declared unalienable. John Adams, one of the drafters of the Declaration of Independence, alienated the right to speak freely and express dissenting views when, as president, he enforced the Alien and Sedition Acts against his political opponents—with Hamilton's support.[63] (Perhaps Hamilton's God had not given "sacred rights" to Jeffersonians!) Another of the drafters, Jefferson himself, alienated the

---

61 Quoted in Ron Chernow, *Alexander Hamilton* (New York: Penguin, 2004), p. 60.

62 Alessandra Stanley, "Understanding the President and His God," *New York Times*, April 29, 2004, p. E1.

63 See David McGowan, "Ethos in Law and History: Alexander Hamilton, The Federalist, and the Supreme Court," 85 *Minnesota Law Review* 755 (2001), pp. 778-779 (noting Hamilton's support, as demonstrated by his reaction to the Virginia and Kentucky resolutions, which opposed the Alien and Sedition acts; among other things, Hamilton recommended using military force to "persuade" Virginia that the Alien and Sedition acts were appropriate).

most basic of rights—to the equal protection of the laws, based on the "truth" that "all men are created equal"—when he helped to write (and strengthen) Virginia's "Slave Code," just a few years after drafting the Declaration of Independence. The revised code denied slaves the right to liberty and to the pursuit of happiness by punishing attempted escape with "outlawry" or death. Jefferson personally suspected that "the blacks . . . are inferior to the whites in the endowments of body and mind." In other words, they were endowed by their Creator not with equality but with inferiority.

There is no right that has not been suspended or trampled during times of crisis and war, even by our greatest presidents. Washington was a strong supporter of the Alien and Sedition acts. Lincoln suspended the writ of habeas corpus, with the approval of Congress. Wilson authorized the "Palmer raids," in which his attorney general seized, arrested, and imprisoned thousands of suspected radicals and aliens in violation of their rights. Roosevelt ordered the detention of more than 100,000 Americans of Japanese descent without even a semblance of due process. He also convened a military tribunal to try—without a jury—an American citizen caught spying for Germany in the United States. And Presidents Truman and Eisenhower, despite their personal dislike of Senator Joseph McCarthy, alienated the rights of political dissidents during the Cold War by enforcing the persecution of Communists, former Communists, and those suspected of leftist sympathies. President George W. Bush violated the due process of detainees—some of whom were Americans—following the terrorist attacks of 9/11.

I wish there were an intellectually satisfying argument for the divine source of rights, as our Founding Fathers tried to put forth. Tactically, that would be the strongest argument liberals could make, especially in America, where many hold a strong belief in an intervening God. But we cannot offer this argument, because many liberals do not believe in concepts like divine hands. We believe in separation of church and state. We are pragmatists, utilitarians, empiricists, secularists, and (God forgive me!) moral relativists.[64] We are skeptical of absolutes (as

64 We are moral relativists only in the sense that, although we believe strongly in certain

George Bernard Shaw cynically quipped: "The golden rule is that there are no golden rules.").

There is no right that is not immune from some alienation or balancing under certain extreme circumstances, such as pandemics or terrorist attacks. Nevertheless, liberals believe strongly in the concept of rights, and in certain specific rights, such as those of equality, due process, freedom of conscience and expression, democratic participation, life, and liberty. I have devoted my life to trying to expand these and other rights and to trying to prevent their alienation. Though I accept the reality that rights can, in fact, diminish in extreme circumstances, the mere possibility that these circumstances may occur should not determine the content of rights during the merely difficult times that challenge every society. It is one of the important functions of rights to prevent (or slow down) popular wrongs during difficult times. Extremes should be regarded not as the norm, but as the exceptions. The slippery slope is not an argument against ever contracting any rights, merely a caution against their too-easy alienation.

It is precisely because liberals reject absolutes and divine endowments that it is so important to make the pragmatic, human-centered, relativistic case for rights.

This question—where do our rights come from?— is crucial, because in the absence of an external, authoritative source of rights, such as God or nature, it is easy to argue that man-made rights must take a backseat to the preferences or perceived needs of the majority in a democracy—which liberals do not accept. Unless there is a compelling source of rights that trumps majoritarian preferences, the default position in a democracy should be a vote of the majority.

Imagine a new democracy being formed on a distant island (or planet). Everyone agrees to begin with the principle of one adult person, one vote. Someone asks, "What about the rights of minorities?" It would then be fair to ask, "Where do these rights come from? Who decides if they exist? What exactly are they? And why should they trump the votes of the majority?"

---

rights and in certain moral principles, we recognize that in truly extraordinary situations, these rights and principles may have to be balanced against the imperative of survival.

The first classic answer is that rights come from a source *external* to law itself, such as nature, God, human instinct, or some other objective reality. This theory (or more precisely, set of theories) is generally called natural law. Our Declaration of Independence explicitly cited natural law—"The laws of Nature and of Nature's God" —as the primary source of the colonists' right to separate from Great Britain.[65] The second classic answer is that rights are *internal* to law—that they are granted by the law itself. This is generally called positive law.

Liberals find it difficult to accept the approach to rights taken by either classic natural law, which is too subjective and open-ended; or classic legal positivism, which is too narrow and closed. I have proposed a third way—an experiential approach based on nurture rather than nature.[66] This approach builds a theory from the bottom up, not from the top down. It constructs this theory by examining the history of injustices, inducing certain experiential lessons, and advocating rights based on those lessons. As a liberal, I come down squarely on the side of nurture, rather than nature, as the primary source of our rights (I would prefer the term "nurtural rights" over "natural rights" if it were more pleasing to the ear).

The great fifteenth-century Jewish commentator Isaac Abarbanel once observed that "experience is more forceful than logic" —or, as Justice Oliver Wendell Holmes later put it: "The life of the law has not been logic; it has been experience." I would state it a bit differently: Neither logic nor experience alone is sufficient. Without a basis in experience, logic is hollow and directionless, but without logic, experience is omni-directional and subject to varying implications. Good logic must be used to derive appropriate lessons from bad experiences.[67]

---

65 It had little choice, since revolution is an extra-legal remedy that cannot be justified by reference to existing "positive" law. See Chapter 6, *infra*. The Declaration also relied on experience, citing the wrongs done to the colonists by the king. In 1689, the English Declaration of Rights had invoked the "known law and statutes" of Great Britain as a source of rights, but those very laws were being used, nearly a century later, to inflict grievous wrongs on the American colonists.

66 Alan Dershowitz, *Rights from Wrongs* (New York: Basic Books, 2005).

67 John Hart Ely put it this way: "Technically, of course, reason alone can't tell you anything: it can only connect premises to conclusions." Ely, *Democracy and Distrust: A Theory of Judicial Review* (Cambridge: Mass.: Harvard University Press, 1980), p. 56. I

A liberal approach to rights posits that it is not necessary to have a conception of the "perfect," the "best," or even the "good" society in order to decide whether rights in general, or certain rights in particular, will serve the ends of a given society. Aristotle was wrong when he argued that we cannot define rights without first determining "the nature of the most desirable way of life." It is enough to have a conception—or consensus—about least desirable ways of life, the very bad society, and about the wrongs that made it so. Based on this experience with wrongs, rights can be designed to prevent (or at least slow down) the recurrence of such wrongs.

There is a real advantage in building a system of rights on acknowledged wrongs rather than on idealized perfection. We will never achieve consensus over what constitutes the best, or even good society. For example, Americans will never agree on whether a pure meritocracy is better than a society based on narrowing the gaps between economic, racial, and other groups. We will continue to disagree about the virtues and vices of capitalism and socialism. We will not agree about whether we would be a better society if more of us went to church and based our actions on faith, or if we were to live life based more on reason and science.[68] We will never agree on the perfect balance between today's economic needs and tomorrow's environmental imperatives. Nor is there consensus regarding whether it is better for the planet to be hermetically divided into nation-states or to move closer to a one-world government.

But there is widespread agreement that we never want to see a recurrence of the Holocaust, the Stalinist mass murders, the Cambodian and Rwandan genocides, slavery, Jim Crow, lynchings, the Inquisition, or the detention of more than 100,000 Japanese Americans.[69] Most reasonable people regard terrorism directed against civilians as unjust, especially after the attacks on 9/11. While there is no complete consensus regarding the lessons to be drawn from this awful history, our

---

would add that it can help structure a process by which we derive rights from experience.

68 See Robert Reich, "The Last Word," *The American Prospect*, July 1, 2004.

69 We have officially apologized for this disgraceful action and paid reparations, despite the Supreme Court having approved it as constitutional.

collective experiences with injustice constitute a fruitful foundation on which to build a liberal theory of rights.[70]

It is more realistic to try to build a theory of rights on the agreed-upon wrongs of the past that we want to avoid repeating, than to try to build such a theory on idealized conceptions of the perfect society, about which we will never agree. Moreover, a theory of rights as an experiential reaction to wrongs is more empirical, observable, and debatable, and less dependent on un-provable faith, metaphor, and myth, than theories premised on sources external to human experience. At bottom, therefore, a theory of rights from wrongs is more democratic and less elitist than divine or natural law theories. It is also more truthful and honest, because rights are not *facts* of nature, like Newton's Laws, waiting somewhere "out there" to be *discovered*, deduced, or intuited. All theories of natural or divine rights are legal fictions created by human beings to satisfy the perceived need for an external and eternal source of rights to check the wrongs produced by human nature and positive law. They are sometimes benevolent fictions, but they are fictions nonetheless, and no amount of need can convert them into fact. Moreover, the fictions of natural and divine rights may be used for malevolent as well as for benevolent purposes. In any event, the reality is that rights are legal constructs devised by the minds of human beings, based on human experience, and they must be consistently defended in the court of public opinion. Any liberal theory of rights must grow out of humanity's experiences with wrongs or injustices.

My liberal theory of experiential (or nurtural) rights is, in a nutshell, the following:

- Rights *do not come from God*, because God does not speak to human beings in a single voice, and rights should exist even if there is no God.

70 My approach does not require unanimous or even near-unanimous acceptance of these or any other events as perfect injustice. For example, I once encountered an eminent professor who actually tried to defend the Crusades! It quickly became apparent that he was abysmally ignorant of the facts concerning the mass slaughter of Jews, Muslims, and heathens, including thousands of babies and children. Thus, I cannot state my view more than **conditionally**: for those who wish to try to prevent a recurrence of events like these, the entrenchment of certain rights will prove useful.

- Rights *do not come from nature*, because nature is value neutral.
- Rights *do not come from the law alone*, because if they did, there would be no basis on which to judge a given legal system. (The case for positive law was considerably weakened by Nazi Germany's use of law to oppress and murder.)
- Rights *do not come from logic*, because there is little consensus about the a priori premises from which rights may be deduced.
- Rights *come from human experience*, particularly experience with injustice. We learn from the mistakes of history that a rights-based system and certain fundamental rights—such as freedom of expression, freedom of and from religion, equal protection of the laws, due process, and participatory democracy—are essential to avoid repetition of the grievous injustices of the past. Working from the bottom up, dystopian view of our experiences with injustice, rather than from the top down, utopian theory of perfect justice, we build rights on a foundation of trial, error, and our uniquely human ability to learn from our mistakes in order to avoid replicating them.[71]

Since liberals do not believe that rights exist outside of human experience—they are not God-given, natural, or eternal—we can do no more than advocate them. I have always believed that the best defense of rights is an active and persistent advocacy, rather than a passive recourse to "higher authority." Every day poses new challenges to entrenched ideologies and new opportunities to advocate rights. The struggle for rights, like the struggle for liberty, never stays won.

If rights can expand based on changing experiences, so too can they contract. The virtue of a static theory of rights is that it never justifies contraction. The vice of a static approach is that it never allows for the expansion of the rights to confront growing wrongs, or the adaptation of old rights to new wrongs. It is like a long-term fixed

71 This ability to derive lessons from mistake, though limited to humans (at least for long-term lessons) has certainly not always been taken advantage of by our species. We often repeat the mistakes of the past and suffer consequences. See George Santayana, *The Life of Reason: Reason in Common Sense* (New York: Dover, 1980), p. 284.

mortgage that neither raises nor lowers your payments in response to changing interest rates.

Those who argue for "evolving" rights, such as the late Justice William J. Brennan, criticized Justice Antonin Scalia's static approach as imposing the dead hands of our forefathers on the living law—what might be called "necrocracy." But despite the metaphor of "evolving" rights, the reality is that changes in the law do not always move in one direction.

Justice Scalia insisted that the Constitution and the rights it contains are "dead"; that the Bill of Rights means precisely "what it meant when it was adopted." He argued that this mode of interpretation makes our rights more enduring and "safer."[72]

The challenge of a liberal approach to rights is to persuade the citizenry that experience teaches us that it is generally preferable to change certain fundamental rights in the direction of expansion and adaptation rather than contradiction or inertia. But there are no guarantees. A dynamic approach is a powerful sword, but it most certainly cuts both ways.

Liberals who reject my experiential approach to rights have an obligation to propose alternatives. Without a compelling theory of the source of rights, it would be difficult to argue that liberalism is better than conservatism, radicalism, and other current or historic "isms," as I do in the next chapter.

---

72 Justice Scalia has generally but not always remained true to his approach in certain cases; see, e.g., *Maryland v. Craig*, 497 U.S. 836 (1990) (dissenting opinion) and *Hamdi v. Rumsfeld*, 542 U.S. 507 (2004). In other cases, however, he has voted to contract rights, despite his rhetoric of consistency over time. In virtually no cases has he voted to expand rights, except when such an expansion served his political and ideological agenda. See, e.g., *Bush v. Gore*, 531 U.S. 98 (2000).

CHAPTER 5

Why Liberalism is Better Than Other "isms"

Liberalism, which in the U.S. situates itself generally at a center-left position on the political spectrum,[73] has a proven track record of success in the marketplace of governing theories. Yet it is under constant attack from both the extreme left and the extreme right, each of which appear to be growing in numbers and influence at the expense of centrist liberalism and centrist conservatism.

The long line from radical hard-left to radical hard-right is a bumpy and ever-shifting continuum with many sharp breaks. Along the continuum lie an assortment of conservatives that includes religious fundamentalists, paleocons, neocons, tea partiers, libertarians, and more centrist Eisenhower-Rockefeller-Romney Republicans. Also along the continuum lie an assortment of left-wingers that includes radicals, socialists, progressives, Kennedy liberals, and "Scoop" Jackson-Pat Moynihan's centrist Democrats. Few sharp lines divide one group from the other, but there are real differences in degree, and even in kind, especially at the extremes.

We do not, in the U.S.—as contrasted with Europe—have significant

73 There is no inherent correlation between being a liberal and a leftist. It is theoretically possible for a liberal to disagree with center-left economic perspectives. Libertarians often consider themselves conservative on some issues and liberal on others. As I argued in Chapter 1, there is no authoritative definition of liberalism.

Communist or Fascist parties or organizations, though some on our far, far left resemble old line Communists, while some on our far, far right are not so different from European fascists.[74] We did, of course, have the Ku Klux Klan, which was (and, in its tiny remaining incarnations, is) an overtly racist organization, as anyone observing the deadly demonstrations in Charlottesville must recognize. We still have some right-wing militia and survivalist groups that engage in violent anti-government activities, as well as anti-Semitism, racism, and xenophobia. And finally, there are the violent and often mentally unstable Jew-haters who shoot up synagogues and other places where Jews congregate. These are extraordinarily dangerous groups that must be investigated, prosecuted, and stopped. The good news is that law enforcement understands these dangers and has the tools necessary to respond, if often imperfectly. Unlike at other times and places in history, our government is trying to protect the *victims* of neo-Nazi and other right-wing extremist violence, rather than the *perpetrators*. These bigots are as marginal as the few violent left wing groups—such as the Weathermen and Black Panthers—that have occasionally made brief appearances on the American scene, along more recently with Antifa.[75] The continuum of our political landscape begins and ends, for the most part, with non-violent radicals of the hard-right and hard-left. Pat Buchanan and Noam Chomsky personify the extremes of today's "acceptable" hard-right and hard-left ideology. It is no accident that both devote much of their attention to demonizing Israel.

As I explained in an earlier chapter, it may be easier for liberals to describe their differences with these other groups than to define the

---

74 There was a time in our early to mid-20th century history when we had small but active Communist and Fascist parties, but they rarely had significant impacts on national elections. The Ku Klux Klan did have passing influence.

75 The New Black Panthers were formed in 1989 and have been designated as a "hate group" by the United States Commission on Civil Rights and the Southern Poverty Law Center. They should not be confused with The Black Panthers from the 1960's. History.com Editors, "Black Panthers," https://www.history.com/topics/civil-rights-movement/black-panthers, (Last updated, March 5, 2020). The Weathermen were considered "the most famous American radical group committed to political violence in the late 1960's and early 1970's.America's." Arthur M. Eckstein, "How the Weather Underground Failed at Revolution and Still Changed the World," *Time* Magazine, November 2, 2016.

"essence"—if there is a singular "essence"—of political, economic, and philosophical liberalism. True liberals share much in common with classic centrist conservatives to the right of them, as well as with some, but certainly not all, progressives to the left of them. Consider for example, the British Conservative Party, which supports a woman's right to choose, gay marriage, separation of church and state, reasonable gun control, opposition to the death penalty, and a strong commitment to freedom of expression. But it also supports economic policies that generally favor the wealthy over the working class.

When I gave a speech to British Conservative Parliamentarians, I was repeatedly asked why I was still a liberal, when conservatives were closer than many leftists to my views on Israel, free speech, due process, and some other issues. I responded that the conservative-liberal divide in my country was very different than in Britain. In the United States, it is difficult to find more than a few Republicans or conservative candidates who represent the views of the British Conservative Party with regard to civil rights. There used to be such a group of "Rockefeller" Republicans, but they cannot today compete in Republican primaries, which push candidates way to the right. I have written elsewhere about how the Supreme Court's decision in *Roe v. Wade*, which constitutionalized a woman's right to choose abortion, "helped secure the presidency for Ronald Reagan by giving him a 'free' issue." It was free because he—and other right-to-life Republicans—could strongly oppose all abortion without alienating moderate Republican women and men who favored a woman's right to choose but felt secure in the knowledge that the Supreme Court would continue to protect that right, regardless of what Reagan and others said or did. Abortion thus became the most important issue for right-wing religious zealots and a marginal issue for moderate Republicans, who favored a woman's right to choose, but who also supported the Republicans' economic and other programs. This helped to destroy the moderate wing of the Republican Party (the so-called Rockefeller Republicans) and drove former moderates (such as the elder George Bush) to the right. (He started as a pro-choice

Republican and ended up as a right-to-life Republican whose hands were tied by the Supreme Court.[76])

A British Parliamentarian asked if I were a Brit, would I vote Conservative? That would depend on who the opposition would be. I would vote for Tony Blair, of the Labor Party, because he too supported individual rights, while at the same time promoting more egalitarian economic policies with which I am more comfortable. But I could not support the then-leader of the Labor Party—Jeremy Corbyn—who is a radical leftist with strong anti-Israel, anti-American, and anti-Libertarian political views. I would more likely vote for conservative politicians such as David Cameron, George Osborne, or Boris Johnson. But I vote in the U.S., not the U.K., and here, my options are more limited. Michael Bloomberg showed that he could win as a Republican or Independent in New York City, but not as a Democrat, Republican, or Independent nationally. Even Eric Cantor wasn't far right enough to survive a Republican primary in Virginia.

A similar phenomenon was at work with regard to the Democratic party in the 2016 presidential primaries, as Bernie Sanders pushed Hillary Clinton away from describing herself as a centrist "liberal" and more toward branding herself as a "progressive who gets things done." The same has been true of the 2020 primary season, in which Sanders pushed more centrist Democrats leftward. Thus, both centrist liberals and centrist conservatives—who together may well constitute a majority or at least plurality of voting Americans—have been marginalized by the current political system, especially the primaries, in which relatively few people vote.

The current situation on university campuses provides another example that situates classic liberals and conservatives closer to each other on the continuum than either is to the extreme left or right. On many campuses, we are seeing centrist liberals and conservatives making common cause against censorial radicals of the extreme left and dogmatic religious fundamentalists of the extreme right. To be sure, there are many more vocal and influential hard-leftists than hard-rightists, especially among liberal arts faculties and students. And so the

76 Dershowitz, *Supreme Injustice*. (Oxford, 2001), pp. 191-197.

common cause is largely a reaction against the political correctness demands for safe-spaces and censorship from left-wing faculty and students and against timid administrators who lack courage to stand up to these assaults on academic freedom and a single standard of fairness and justice.

It is perhaps ironic that although the political divide among elected officials is somewhat narrower in Great Britain than it is in the U.S. (with the exception of Jeremy Corbyn), the academic divide among university students and faculty in Britain is far wider. The academic hard-left is quite vocal on both sides of the Atlantic, but it is far stronger and more deeply entrenched in British universities than in our own. We have many loud extremists, especially on the hard-left, but they still represent a relatively small, though influential, segment of student bodies throughout the country.

There are many reasons for this difference, such as the influence of trade unions, which in Great Britain tend to be on the far left. American unions have little influence on academic life here, though academic associations—such as the National Women's Studies Association, the American Studies Association, the Critical Ethnic Studies Association, the African Literature Association, National Association of Chicana and Chicano Studies, Native American and Indigenous Studies Association, and Librarians and Archivists with Palestine—have adopted many hard-left positions, particularly against Israel. British universities also have considerably higher percentages of students and faculty of Muslim and Arab background than do most American universities, and many of these academics create coalitions with hard-leftists, particularly with regard to protests against Israel, the United States, and "colonialism." This new form of coalition building has been given the pretentious name "intersectionality," which deliberately masks the lack of agreement among groups that have little in common beyond their hatred of Israel and the United States, their perceived victimization, and their disdain for civil discourse.

The reality is that as a liberal, I have far more in common—on the campus, in the voting booth, and in life—with classic conservatives than I do with hard-left radicals. This is true not only with regard to Israel—which is both a symptom and a cause of our differences—but also with regard to freedom of expression, identity politics, tolerance of differing views, radical redistribution of wealth, foreign policy, criminal justice reform, and due process (especially with regard to fairness to students accused of sexual assault and harassment), and a range of other issues, both practical and ideological. That is why I am hated by the far left far more than by centrist conservatives and even by some on the hard-right. My speeches are picketed and disrupted by radical leftists, while evangelical rightists listen politely and disagree. When I spoke to thousands of students at Liberty University—a Baptist school—I was treated politely, even when I expressed my strong views about choice and gay marriage.

As a liberal, I also have much in common with *some* people who call themselves "progressives." The old divide between "liberals" and "progressives"—who, when I was growing up, included Communists, Socialists, and others well to the left of liberals—has narrowed. The defining moment, for me and I suspect others like me, came with the widespread support received by Bernie Sanders during the 2016 and 2020 primary seasons. Never before in my lifetime had so radical a leftist and so anti-Israel a candidate receive so much support from Democrats. The fact that he was a Jew did not ameliorate the concerns. Sanders has always been an uncompromising radical and a socialist. That's why he never got anything done as a Senator. Hillary Clinton and Joe Biden were classic centrist liberals, whether or not they chose to use that word to describe their views. There were real differences between Sanders and his major opponents. But the primaries brought them closer together. Sanders became more of a New Deal Democrat, whose views—at least those he publicly expressed—were more akin to those of FDR and Ted Kennedy than to Norman Thomas or Henry Wallace. His utopias were the Scandinavian countries, not the Soviet Union, Cuba, Venezuela, or China—though he foolishly praised these failed communist tyrannies for some of their accomplishments (much as fascist apologists praised Mussolini for making the trains run on time).

It is noteworthy that in the course of the debates between Sanders and his opponents, no one claimed the mantle of "liberal." Sanders accused them of not being progressive because of the sources of some of their campaign contributions and speaking fees, as well as some of their positions regarding Wall Street, health care, and other "litmus test" issues. (Hypocritically, Sanders's own right-wing position on gun control reflects his need to placate gun-owning contributors and voters in his state.) Sanders's opponents responded by arguing that Sanders's particularistic definition of progressive would exclude such iconic progressives as Ted Kennedy, Walter Mondale, Mike Dukakis, George McGovern, and Hubert Humphrey, as well as President Obama. But, in making this argument, they didn't use the word "liberal" in characterizing these self-described liberals. Nor did they accuse Sanders of not being a liberal, or themselves claim that mantle. It is as if being labeled a liberal is a kiss of death, not only for Republican aspirants, but also for those seeking votes in Democratic primaries. This is an ominous development.

Some pundits have observed that the Democratic Party is being pushed to the left by young voters, and that Sanders's relatively strong showings, both in 2016 and 2020, is a symptom of that development. Others say that it is Sanders's personal characteristics—his long commitment to progressive causes, his obvious sincerity, and his down-to-earth style—that have persuaded young people to support him and follow his progressive policies. There is obviously some truth in both perspectives. But the reality remains that hardly anyone in politics—not even obvious liberals like Hillary Clinton and Joe Biden—wants to be labeled a liberal. "A progressive who gets things done" is the newest euphemism for a centrist liberal who wants to preserve and improve most existing institutions and is willing to acknowledge political realities that often require compromise to achieve half a loaf instead of deadlock. But the fact that liberal candidates need a euphemism under which to cover their pragmatic liberalism is a sad commentary on today's politics. No one claims the mantle of "liberal," though several—including Joe Biden—express views and support policies that fit that label.

I was Elizabeth Warren's colleague on the Harvard Law School faculty for several years. Back then, she was far more of a centrist liberal, but Sanders pushed her leftward, which may well have cost her the nomination and presidency. The American voting public is closer to the old Warren than to the newly minted and Sanders-influenced Warren. It will be interesting to watch how she reacts to the electoral failures she suffered, even in her home-state primary.

Most liberals and progressives—particularly those seeking high elected office—have similar ideological goals. They seek to achieve: the broadest possible health care coverage; the most affordable educational opportunities; the fairest possible tax policy; the most effective constraints on Wall Street, big banks and giant corporations; the best possible way to reduce the influence of money on politics; the most reasonable methods for protecting the environment from climate change; the most efficient programs to grow the economy, create jobs and raise wages; the best possible balance between protecting us against terrorism, while preserving our civil liberties; the fairest possible road to citizenship for undocumented people living and working among us; the toughest possible deterrence against Iran developing a nuclear arsenal, short of military action; the preservation of a strong Israel, capable of defending itself from terrorist and other threats, while pressuring the nation-state of the Jewish people to stop settlement activity and move toward a two-state solution; the maintenance of America's superior military might, without using it except when our national security is directly threatened; the refusal to discriminate against, demonize, stereotype, or profile any religious, ethnic, or national origin group based on what some in the group have done; the doing of everything reasonable to reduce the number of deaths among young African Americans at the hands of police; and the implementation of effective controls that keep guns out of the hands of criminals, terrorists, the mentally ill, and violence-prone individuals; the most effective way, consistent with basic liberties, to prevent the spread of pandemics and to rebuild our economy.

Most liberals and progressives (as well as many centrist-conservatives) agree on these and other desirable ends. The disagreement is largely over means, including trade-offs, prioritization, and political compromises. Liberals tend to want to preserve most existing institutional structures—such as Obamacare, Social Security, prisons, and immigration agencies—while improving them in an effort to bring us closer to the desired ends. Progressives tend to be willing to dismantle at least some of these institutions in the hope that they can achieve fundamental structural reform.

In general, liberals are more concerned about means, processes, and balances than progressives, who tend to focus more on utopic ends. The Democratic primary battles between Sanders and his opponents in 2016 and 2020, though they moved Sanders slightly closer to the center on several issues, illustrated some important differences between liberals and progressives, especially with regard to health care, college tuition, taxation, trade agreements, banking reform, and immigration. It also demonstrated the vast differences between Democratic candidates, on the one hand, and nearly all the Republican candidates on the other hand. Rarely has the gulf between Democrats and Republicans been so wide on issues ranging from health care, to immigration, to gay marriage, to abortion, to the role of the Supreme Court, to climate change, to the Iran deal, to taxation, to dealing with pandemics, to gun control and gun rights, to the role of religion in governance, and to use of the military in the war against terrorism. Democratic and Republican primaries may not have afforded voters distinct choices among intra-party candidates, but the general election affords some of the biggest differences in policies between the Democratic and Republican nominees. Our differences have only grown bigger with the election of Donald Trump.

In some respects, the 2020 primary season has been the reverse mirror image of 2016. In 2016, the Republicans had numerous candidates reflecting different strands of the right, from centrist conservatives to hard-right reactionaries to a non-ideological populist (who ultimately won). The Democrats had a party favorite, challenged by an outsider. In 2020, the Democrats had numerous candidates, while the Republicans have an incumbent, with no serious competition.

The differences both within and between parties will keep me a Democrat for the foreseeable future. I am surely not alone in advocating the liberal agenda, while expressing concern about the leftward trend of the Democratic Party. Many citizens of all ages are uncomfortable with the stark choice between the radical left and the reactionary right. We want to preserve but improve such institutions as the free market economy, social security, Obamacare, the current election system, and the progressive income tax. We want change, but not "revolution."

We are not fans of "the Squad," with their radical views on both domestic and foreign policy, though we recognize that they represent a changing dynamic among some elements of the Democratic Party. We want to make sure that their radical ideas remain marginalized, without alienating young people who support some of them.

The current lineup may, of course, change over time. We may see the return of moderate conservatives to the mainstream of the Republican Party, especially if the Party were to experience the kind of cataclysmic defeat in 2020 it suffered when it selected Barry Goldwater to be its presidential nominee back in 1964. He carried only six states and received 38.5 of the popular vote. At that time, Goldwater represented the extreme right wing of the Republican Party. Today he would be closer to the center.

The same might have been true if the Democrats had nominated a radical like Sanders and experienced the same kind of defeat suffered by Senator George McGovern in 1972. McGovern, a liberal closer to the center than Sanders, carried one state and received 37.5 percent of the popular vote, producing the widest electoral margin in modern history.

When it became clear in 2016 that Sanders could not win the nomination, I wrote an op-ed warning Hillary Clinton against moving too far to the left in an effort to court Sanders's voters. I argued that Sanders was more dangerous losing the nomination than he would have been as the Democratic nominee.

> "Had Sanders won the nomination, he would likely have been demolished in the general election, as were Michael Dukakis, George McGovern and Walter Mondale who represented the left wing of the Party, but were much closer to the center than he is. Sanders hard-left repressive followers would have been marginalized; as well they should be, because the Democrats can only win as centrist liberals, rather than hard-left radicals. But with Sanders losing the nomination, his power and that of his supporters, increased, because Hil-

> lary Clinton did everything in her power to recruit into her camp, those who continued to 'Feel the Bern.' That empowered not only the real progressives who supported Sanders, but also the repressives who falsely hide their true anti-liberal views under the ill-fitting cloak of progressivism. These repressives have little tolerance for differing viewpoints and seek to shut down speakers who refuse to tow their 'politically correct line.'"

I cautioned that Clinton would be smart to resist the temptation to move leftward once she had secured the Democratic nomination. I urged her to run as a "liberal," which is, in fact, what she is—a centrist liberal who rejects revolution and the radical dismantling of imperfect institutions, such as Obamacare. Like her husband, she should have remained at the liberal center, both on domestic and foreign policy issues. That has always been the winning strategy for Democrats, and the Sanders' brushfire should not have changed that successful approach.

I argued that if Clinton felt the need to move to the far left, she might succeed in the short run in keeping some of Sanders' supporters from staying home on Election Day, but she would risk alienating centrist, independent, and undecided voters, who determine the outcome of most national elections. I pointed out that it was likely that many of Sanders's supporters would come out and vote for Clinton, though some who want to shake up the system might support Trump. Far-left zealots, who hate liberals even more than they hate conservatives, might stay home, but their numbers are relatively small, despite the loud noises they emit. Moreover, there is nothing Clinton could have done to satisfy the far-left repressives who want to overthrow existing institutions and suppress speech they deem incorrect. These intolerant extremists reject the idea that respect be accorded even to those with whom they disagree.

I think the same thing is true today in regard to Biden. It is important to understand that the differences between liberal candidates such as Biden, and far left Sanders supporters, are not merely matters of degree on many important issues. They are matters of kind. Biden wants realistic improvements in existing institutions, such as health care, capital markets, banking, the military, our education system, and other structures. Sanders and his far-left followers want revolutionary dismantling of these and other existing institutions. His most radical supporters want even more revolutionary structural changes that would destabilize and weaken our nation. It is not that Sanders's most radical supporters are idealists whose ideas are good but unrealistic, and Biden a pragmatist whose ideas are compromises with their more radical ideals. Biden is right and they are wrong about many issues over which they disagree. And Biden should stick to his guns, as should other liberals.

It is understandable that in order to secure the endorsements of Sanders, Warren, Alexandria Ocasio-Cortez, and other progressives, Biden would have to endorse some of their less-radical and more realistic proposals, which he has done. But it would be a mistake to move so far to the left as to lose the votes of more centrist voters in swing states.

Mainstream American voters want evolution, not revolution. We want stability, predictability, and gradual improvements. We don't want to see the U.S. emulate Europe, where the political pendulum often swings widely between the left and the right and where extremist parties of both the hard-left and hard-right are growing in influence. We prefer narrower pendulum swings of the kind seen when President Bill Clinton replaced the first President Bush.

Democracy thrives at the center and suffers when extremists are not marginalized. History has shown that nations caught between the brown of hard-right extremism and the red of hard-left extremism often choose poorly and suffer grave consequences. Moreover, as I will show in the next chapter, our system of checks and balances and tripartite division of powers works best when both parties move away from extremes and closer to the center. Liberalism is better for America and more consistent with its enduring values than radicalism.

Although today's voters may be no more extreme than voters in the past, our primary system rewards both Democratic and Republican extremists, because so few centrists vote. The general election, on the other hand, with many more voters, generally rewards centrists who promise improvement and stability. The 2020 race may not tell us much about the future of American politics. Most Democratic primary voters seemed more interested in nominating a candidate who they believed could defeat President Trump than a candidate about whom they were enthusiastic. The candidate they settled on tells us more about the dynamics of *this* election than about future trends.

Only time and new elections will tell what the political landscape will look like in generations to come, or even in the current election cycle. In the long run, it may be useful to try to reconfigure the current breakdown between right and left along a somewhat different continuum—one that focuses on basic freedoms and civil liberties, rather than on the conventional distinction between Democrats (who include liberals, as well as progressives and left-wing radicals) and Republicans (who include centrist supporters of individual liberty, as well as radical right-wingers and religious fundamentalists who subordinate liberty to submission to God's will).

On one pole of this new continuum would be liberals and libertarian conservatives, and on the other pole would be radical leftists and fundamentalist conservatives. This would reflect the reality that although the current Democratic left has enormous differences with the current Republican right, in many respects the hard-left has more in common ideologically and methodologically with the hard-right than either does to centrist liberals and conservatives. Both the hard-left and hard-right have little tolerance for dissent because they know the truth, and dissent only strengthens their enemies. Both the hard-left and hard-right are prisoners of their own dogma and do not need science or experience to inform or challenge their fixed ideologies. The hard-right, for example, doesn't care about facts when it comes to climate control, while the hard-left doesn't care about facts when it comes to freedom of speech, due process for students accused of sexual misconduct, or Israel. Both the hard-left and the hard-right want to dismantle existing institutions. The hard-right wants to end the Internal Revenue Service, The Department of Education, The Environmental Protection Agency, and the ATF (Bureau of Alcohol, Tobacco, Firearms and Explosives). The hard-left wants to replace Obamacare with universal healthcare, abolish ICE, eliminate nuclear weapons (and much of the military), end most imprisonment, and curtail due process for accused sex offenders. Centrist-liberals and conservatives want to preserve these and other governmental institutions and processes while changing them to make them comport better with their liberal and conservative policies.

The alliances that are currently forming on university campuses between centrist liberals and conservatives in defense of freedom of expression and in opposition to identity politics may endure and enter the political mainstream as the current generation of students becomes political, media, economic, and cultural leaders. That would be a healthy development. The alternative—a nation torn between the illiberal extremes of the radical left and reactionary right—would endanger our rights, our liberties, and our security.

It is a common mistake to believe that the liberal (or center) left is merely a compromise with the radical (or hard) left, who are the purists of progressive policies.

Friends on the hard-left often try to compliment me by saying, in a somewhat condescending way, that my liberal views will "evolve" into their radical "truths." I, too, will become "politically correct," when I realize that liberalism is merely a waystation on the road to radicalism—when I become "woke."

My centrist conservative friends describe similar conversations with members of the radical or religious right. They, too, are seen as compromisers on the road to pure truth.

The fundamental error made by these left- and right-wing extremists is to deny the authenticity of centrist positions and to insist that the only authentically left- and right-wing views are on the extreme ends of the political spectrum. But the liberal center has its own independent claims to authenticity. Liberalism is qualitatively different from—and, in my view, better than—radicalism. We liberals are not merely pseudo-radicals who haven't yet reached the hard-left radical or progressive nirvana.

We are where we want to be, thank you. And we don't need to be patronized by those who have gone further along the spectrum of the left. As to certain issues—such as health care, student debt, affordable higher education, fairer taxation—we can learn from the hard-left and adapt and even adopt. But, as to other fundamental issues—such as freedom of expression and due process—we deny it is a spectrum: the hard-left is substantively and qualitatively at war with centrist-liberals when it comes to these issues. We don't want to "evolve" into Stalinist censors and persecutors who do not believe that opposing viewpoints need to be heard. We believe not only that liberals are right on these issues, but that the radical left is dead wrong. Liberalism is better than radicalism. We must defend liberalism on its own merits.

Many of those who voted for Sanders are decent people who truly deserve to be called "progressives." But among his most active supporters were hard-left elements within organizations such as CodePink, MoveOn, Antifa, Jewish Voice for Peace, and some elements of Black Lives Matter, who are more appropriately called repressives. Too many of them have too little tolerance for views different than their own.

Traditional liberals who have made their home in the Democratic Party should be wary of those groups. Much like the Sanders campaign, many of them are dominated by veterans of Occupy Wall Street and other radical groups whose brand of unfocused revolutionary politics is widely derided by mainstream Democrats and Republicans alike. They are at war with certain core liberal values, particularly as regards free speech and due process for thee as well as for me. History proves that our values are more enduring and more consistent with democracy. And we must say so.

Dozens of Black Lives Matter activists infiltrated Donald Trump rallies and forced the organizers to cancel due to security concerns after they became involved in heated confrontations with Trump's supporters. Whatever one may think of Trump's policies, there is no excuse for preventing the candidate from expressing them at a political rally. They abridged both Trump's right to free expression and the ability of thousands of their fellow citizens to participate in the political process. MoveOn thanked the disruptors for their actions.

Nor were such repressive actions confined to Trump rallies: Democratic events have regularly been targeted as well. In Philadelphia, during the 2016 campaign, Black Lives Matter activists engaged in a lengthy confrontation with former President Bill Clinton, repeatedly shouting over his attempts to engage them in substantive discussion. Similar confrontations have taken place during the 2020 primary season.

These repressive tactics have been on clearest display in the context of the debate surrounding the Israeli-Palestinian conflict. Far-left activism organized by BLM shut down an LGBTQ conference in Chicago by storming the event and denying speakers the opportunity to address the crowd, by chanting "occupy, occupy" and "no justice, no peace." While protests are a legitimate part of the political process, disruptive efforts to shut down speakers are not.[77]

Disruptive tactics have gone hand in hand with other initiatives designed to silence pro-Israel voices. CodePink, many of the leaders of Black Lives Matter, and a host of other organizations have endorsed or cooperated with the Boycott, Divestment, and Sanctions movement against Israel and Zionists. Among other measures, BDS calls for the boycotting of Israeli cultural and academic institutions, as well as for "common sense" boycotts of Jewish individuals and organizations that are too supportive of Israel. I am on the list of speakers to be boycotted and shouted down.[78]

On university campuses, repressives have justified silencing dissent using "safe space" language, arguing that students should not be exposed to ideas or historical facts that they find threatening. This demonstrates a profoundly warped conception, or outright rejection, of free speech and academic freedom. They should read John Stuart Mill—and Martin Luther King.

The conflicts between liberals and repressive hard-left radicals have parallels in the relationship between centrist conservatives and the hard-right: on certain issues—such as the economy—they may be

---

77 Milo Yiannopoulos, a former Breitbart News editor, was evacuated from the campus of Berkeley after a large crowd of protestors—some of which threw rocks and Molotov cocktails at officers—gathered. More recently, University of Penn students denied the former director of ICE, Thomas Homan, his right to speak by loudly chanting "go home." And, a University of California #SpeechMatters2020 conference was disrupted by protestors standing in front of speakers while constantly interrupting them.

78 Sanders himself contributed to anti-Israel defamation: In an interview with the editorial board of the *New York Daily News*, he suggested that 10,000 civilians had been killed in Gaza by Israel during Operation Protective Edge, and that Israel's responses to terror rockets and tunnels has been "disproportionate." The truth is that somewhere between 600 and 1,500 civilians—many of whom were used as human shields by Hamas—were killed in a legitimate military effort to protect Israeli civilians, despite Israeli efforts to minimize civilian casualties. He has accused Israeli leaders of racism and denial of human rights. Such woeful misrepresentations serve to justify and encourage the repressive bigotry that has become the staple of anti-Israel, left-wing activists.

on a political spectrum or continuum. But on other issues—such as separation of church and state, gay and abortion rights, and freedom of expression—there is a fundamental disconnect with the hard-right, most especially the religious hard-right. Real conservatives don't want to "evolve" into fundamentalists who believe we should be governed by the Bible rather than the Constitution.

Here again, the center-left (liberals) and the center-right (libertarians and economic conservatives) share common ideological opponents on the hard-left and hard-right. We believe that *both* extremes endanger American values and stability. We also believe they are incompatible with true liberal and conservative ideologies. They are not merely different in degree from us, they are different in kind, and in negative ways.

That's why it is important to make the case for centrism in a positive and persuasive way, not as a compromise with some pure vision of left or right-wing extreme truth, but as an independently standing political position. And that's why it's equally important to make the case *against* extremism on both the left and the right, not as matter-of-degree, but rather as independent dangers to be combatted in the marketplace of ideas.

Liberals must be open to hearing, adapting, and adopting some of the positive new ideas of radicals, such as those relating to health care, affordable higher education, and fairer taxation. But we must stand strong against their repressive ideology regarding free speech, due process, and identity politics.

The case for the center, particularly for the center-left—for liberalism—is a difficult case to make, especially among those young people, students, and academics who tend to see grey-area issues as black and white, and who eschew nuance, complexity, and the need to balance conflicting claims to the truth. For them, there is only one truth, and it lies on the extreme ends of any continuum. For them, all politics is movement toward these extremes, and anyone who is not on the road to their ultimate truth is a traitor, a heretic, a knave, or a fool. The center is inauthentic, unless it is merely a waystation on the road to their political nirvana.

We must reclaim the authenticity of centrist liberalism as a *goal*, and not merely as a means toward their unacceptable ends. We must articulate, develop, and defend a philosophy of centrist liberalism, not as a compromise with authentic radicalism, but as a legitimate stand-alone product in the marketplace of ideas. We should express pride in our liberalism and advertise and sell our product so as to compete and win in the open competition of ideas. We have the winning arguments and the historical evidence on our side. We must persuade the American public that centrism is most compatible with our constitutional and moral values. It is to these issues that I now turn.

CHAPTER 6

The U.S. Constitution is a Centrist Document Designed to Promote Centrist Governance

The Constitution is a centrist document, born of moral and political compromises, based on a separation of powers, checks and balances, and a division of authority between the federal and state governments. It established a republic with structural innovations designed to impose centrist constraints on the potential for extremism that the Framers feared would inhere in a direct, popular, democracy—which they rejected. It prescribes neither liberalism nor conservatism as a governing philosophy, though it contains elements of both, while eschewing extremism.

We tend to think of the Constitution and Declaration of Independence as similar documents of liberty. Sometimes they are even confused. When I wrote a book about the Declaration of Independence—*America Declares Independence*—the publisher mistakenly used words from the Constitution ("We the people...") on the cover of the book. When I showed the cover to several of my colleagues without alerting them to the error and asked them for their opinion of the aesthetics, no one noticed it. But in fact, these two documents are as different—conceptually, morally, legally, and politically—as any two documents of liberty could possibly be.

The Declaration of Independence is an extremist, radical, revolutionary, lawless manifesto of rebellion. It relies on God, natural unwritten law, morality, "self-evident" propositions, and unalienable rights. The Constitution, on the other hand, is a relatively conservative legal document. Its most important structural innovations–the separation of powers, checks and balances, and federalism–limited the power of any one governmental entity. It sets out rules, structures, positive written laws, and a difficult process for amending. The body of the Constitution contains two individual rights–against ex post facto laws and bills of attainder–both of which are really structural limitations on the power of the legislature. It also protects against "impairing the obligation of contracts." And the Fifth Amendment prohibits the taking of private property for public use "without just compensation"–provisions which would make it difficult for Socialism or Fascism to take root. The Constitution does not invoke God or rely on God's law or the laws of nature. Instead it relies on man-made positive laws, and the consent of "we the people." Indeed, it was criticized by religious leaders at the time as the "godless" Constitution.

There are good reasons for these differences: revolutionaries need God and natural law on the side of their radicalism, because they certainly don't have the written, positive law. But once the revolution has succeeded, there is a need to prevent other revolutionaries from doing to the new republic what the colonists did to Great Britain–namely, revolt and secede based on their conceptions of divine or natural law. As Hannah Arendt once put it: "The most radical revolutionary will become a conservative the day after the revolution."[79]

The erstwhile revolutionaries who drafted and then defended the Constitution were a mix of conservatives, such as Alexander Hamilton and John Adams; moderates, such as George Washington and John Jay; and liberals, like James Madison and Thomas Jefferson (who was out of the country when the Constitution was drafted, but whose influence was palpable). The Constitution they drafted was the pragmatic result of many compromises–among large and small, slaveholding and abolitionist, and rich and poor states–and was intended to endure; it has done so for more than two-and-a-quarter centuries with relatively

79 Hannah Arendt. "Reflection Civil Disobedience." *The New Yorker*, September 12, 1970.

few amendments. The most important of these amendments are the initial ten—the Bill of Rights—which are a mixture of conservative limitations on the power of the federal government ("Congress shall make no law...") and liberal recognition of individual rights ("The right of the people to be secure..."). The body of the Constitution is so conservative that many of its signers conditioned their approval on the promise that a more liberal Bill of Rights would be forthcoming. These first ten amendments were designed to constrain the powers of the federal government and to assure the dominance of the rule of law. They have been interpreted over time to apply to the states, as well as to individuals who act in the name of the state.

The Declaration of Independence, on the other hand, was a radical, treasonous document that accused King George III of the most serious sins and crimes against the colonists. I own the first published British volume that includes the Declaration of Independence as an important state document. It deliberately omits the name of the king for fear that the publisher of the book would be charged with treason. The very act of drafting and publishing the Declaration was a crime, and its signatories would likely have been executed had we lost the Revolutionary War. As Benjamin Franklin wrote: "We must indeed all hang together or, most assuredly, we shall all hang separately."

The Declaration of Independence was a document of advocacy, not law, designed to justify an unlawful rebellion. But it was also a glorious document of aspiration, if not reality. The words "All men are created equal" were written on a table-desk built for Jefferson by one of his slaves. "All men" referred only to property-owning white men. As a description of the situation in the colonies, equality was a lie. As an aspirational document, it helped set the tone for subsequent amendments, legislation, and judicial decisions that have moved us closer to the aspirational goal of real equality.

It took the Fourteenth Amendment, with its "Equal Protection" clause, and the Nineteenth Amendment, granting women equality of the ballot, to turn the rhetoric of the Declaration into binding constitutional law. This reflects the other major difference between the two documents: The Declaration is not a legal document; its words are *not* the law of the land. The Constitution *is* the law, binding on all branches of government and on its citizens. The Declaration articulates the political and moral basis for the Constitution. After declaring that all men are "endowed by their creator with certain unalienable rights," it sets out the conditions for turning these abstract rights into concrete legal protections: "That to secure these rights, governments are instituted among men, deriving their just powers from the consent of the governed"—a centrist concept.

Thomas Jefferson, near the fiftieth anniversary of those words he penned in 1776, wrote the following from his deathbed about the meaning of the Declaration of Independence and the Constitution, not only for Americans, but for the entire world:

> [M]ay it be to the world what I believe it will be, (to some parts sooner, to others later, but finally to all) the signal of arousing men to burst the chains, under which monkish ignorance and superstition had persuaded them to bind themselves, and to assume the blessings and security of self government. [T]he form which we have substituted restores the free right to the unbounded exercise of reason and freedom of opinion. All eyes are opened, or opening to the rights of man. [T]he general spread of the light of science has already laid open to every view the palpable truth that the mass of mankind has not been born, with saddles on their backs, nor a favored few booted and spurred, ready to ride them legitimately by the grace of God. [T]hese are grounds of hope for others. For ourselves let the annual return of this day, for ever refresh our recollections of these rights and an undiminished devotion to them.[80]

No more articulate statement of the liberal perspective has ever been written.

The road from the radical Declaration's unalienable rights to the centrist Constitution and its liberal Bill of Rights was a rocky one, with war and internal conflict intervening. But it was a clear road, with the basis for the Constitution set forth in the Declaration.

Our general stability as a centrist republic—with the dramatic

---

80 Letter from Thomas Jefferson to Roger Weightman, Monticello, June 24, 1826.

exception of the Civil War—is testament to the wisdom of those who drafted and ratified the most enduring Constitution in the history of humankind.

Parliamentary democracies are very different from our republic. They place the legislative, executive, and, in some countries, even the judicial functions under the ultimate control of the Parliament.[81] The Prime Minister is selected by the Parliament and serves at its pleasure, subject to removal by a simple vote of no confidence, as distinguished from our cumbersome impeachment process. Under our Constitution, the functions of government are divided among three separate, equal, and independent branches. Moreover, the President may be of one party and the legislature, which is comprised of two houses, may be under the control of the other party—or may itself be divided, with the Senate and House being controlled by different parties. Finally, although in theory, the judicial branch is supposed to be non-partisan, in practice, the Supreme Court and lower courts can also be dominated by one party. The Supreme Court, with its power of judicial review, has the final word, subject only to constitutional amendment, on the lawfulness of all legislative and executive actions. As the late Justice Robert Jackson once commented on the finality of Supreme Court judgments: "We are not final because we are infallible, but we are infallible only because we are final."

Our complex and often cumbersome system was not designed for efficiency. It was designed to protect against tyranny, including what the Framers feared nearly as much as they feared the absolute power of a monarch—tyranny of the majority. As Jon Meacham put it in his biography of our first populist president, Andrew Jackson: "The men who gathered in Philadelphia in 1787 had not been interested in establishing the rule of the majority. Quite the opposite. [They were] largely concerned how the new nation might most effectively check the popular will...the people, broadly defined, were not to be trusted with too much power."[82] The entire structure of the Constitution and

81 The British House of Lords is part of Parliament, though it has a degree of independence, as does the rest of the judiciary, which is a creation of Parliament, as distinguished from our Supreme Court, which derives its authority from our Constitution.

82 Jon Meacham, *American Lion*, (New York: Random House, 2008), pp. 43 - 44.

the Bill of Rights was designed as a check on "pure" popular, democracy: The President was elected not by the popular vote of the small percentage of Americans who were eligible to cast a ballot, he—and I use the male pronoun advisedly—was selected by a group of Platonic Guardians, called electors. Senators were selected by their state legislatures, not by popular vote, and the smallest and largest states each had two senators, thus diminishing the voting power of citizens of the larger states. Only members of the House of Representatives directly "represented" the people, and even they were elected only by white, male, property-owning citizens, over the age of 21. Judges were nominated by the President and confirmed by the Senate, thus providing some check on the power of the President to control the judiciary. The President could be removed only by a two-thirds vote of the Senate, following an impeachment by a majority of the House.

Some of these limitations on democracy have been modified by amendments, Supreme Court decisions and long–term practices: senators are now elected by the citizens; no citizen over the age of 18 may be denied the vote based on race, gender, or ability to pay a poll tax; the Electoral College is now largely a formality, in which electors are bound to vote for the candidate who received the most votes in the state.[83]

Despite these changes, the structure of the Constitution still promotes centrist governance and policies. Unless all the branches are under the control of the same party, compromises will be required to enact and implement controversial proposals. Such compromises generally move proposals away from extremes and toward the center. That was the intent of the Framers, and, for the most part, that is how it has worked out in most situations throughout our history. The issue of slavery was, of course, the exception, because in the end, and despite decades of effort, it proved impossible to compromise over such a morally divisive issue. A bloody war had to be fought and the Constitution had to be amended.

---

83 There are now efforts to reduce the impact of the Electoral College even further by requiring electors in each state to cast their votes for the candidate who received the most votes *nationally*. This is designed to assure that the winner of the national popular vote receives the most electoral votes.

Most issues that have deeply divided—and still divide our nation—have been resolved by compromises that have left extremists on all sides dissatisfied, but have been deemed acceptable, if not perfect, by the centrist majority. Among these compromises have been the "New Deal" and its progeny, which was not socialist enough for the hard-left, nor capitalist enough for the hard-right; desegregation, which moved too slowly for integrationists and too quickly for segregationists; gun control, which is too controlling for Second Amendment extremists and not controlling enough for those who want to disarm America; women's rights, including access to abortions, which have not gone far enough for many feminists, but too far for religious fundamentalists; separation of church and state, which exists more in constitutional theory than in everyday practice; protection for the environment, which is deemed insufficient by environmental advocates and unnecessary by those who regard climate change as an unscientific exaggeration; healthcare, which some want to see universalized, while others prefer it to be left to the free market; tax and other economic policies, which many believe create unacceptable wealth disparities, while others believe that such disparities "trickle down" and benefit all segments of society; foreign and military policies, which some regard as too "hawkish" and others regard as too "dovish;" criminal justice, which some believe favors the accused over victims, while others believe the opposite. With regard to all of these, and other divisive issues, we have seen compromises that have rejected both extremes and landed close to the middle—although no one agrees precisely what constitutes "the middle" when it comes to strongly held ideological views. All of these controversial policies are works in progress because compromises rarely resolve hotly disputed issues with finality. That, too, is a characteristic of centrist governance.

In the U.S., as contrasted with Europe, the pendulum swings of policies and actions have tended to be relatively narrow, since, historically, the two parties have not been as far apart ideologically as left and right-wing parties have been in Europe. For example, the period between the two world wars saw the rise of Fascism and Communism as competing governing ideologies in several European countries, especially during the Great Depression. In the U.S., on the other hand, FDR's

New Deal was a centrist compromise that weakened the powers of nascent fascist and communist groups and parties. The Constitution's constraints on impairing private contracts and taking private property would have made it more difficult to accept Communism or Fascism, even if the voters had favored such extreme measures, which few did. The centrist tendencies of the American voters may now be changing, but the structural differences may still produce more compromises here than in Europe. They may also cause more gridlock and deadlock, especially with a divided government.

Even when all the branches are controlled by one party, there are constraints on extremism from *within* the party in control, because both the Democrats and Republicans have deep internal divisions, typical of two-party as distinguished from multi-party systems, and reflective of the different regions and states that comprise our electorate. Resolving these divisions pulls governance toward the center in most, though not all, instances.

A counterexample would be the impeachments of Presidents Trump and Clinton. Alexander Hamilton predicted in *The Federalist Papers* No. 65, that impeachments may not be amenable to centrist compromise because they:

> will seldom fail to agitate the passions of the whole community, and to divide it into parties more or less friendly or inimical to the accused. In many cases it will connect itself with the pre-existing factions, and will enlist all their animosities, partialities, influence, and interest on one side or the other; and in such cases there will always be the greatest danger that the decision will be regulated more by the comparative strength of parties than by the real demonstrations of innocence or guilt.

That is why the Framers also included in the Constitution a centrist constraint on extremism in the context of impeachment: the requirement of a two-thirds vote of the Senate for removal. None of the three Presidents who were impeached by a majority vote of the House were removed by two-thirds vote of the Senate, though President Richard

Nixon probably would have been impeached and removed had he not resigned.

Despite all of these structural constraints on extremism, there have been periods in our history during which extremist elements have become influential enough to block change, if not affirmatively to implement their extremist policies. The influence of the Ku Klux Klan managed to prevent—at least for a time—the movement towards racial and gender equality; the Immigration Restriction League halted the flow of Jewish, Italian, Slavic, and other "undesirable races" during the early decades of the 20th century; the America First Movement stopped America's early entry into the two world wars; The John Birch Society and its predecessors slowed down the end of McCarthyism; the National Rifle Association has long prevented reasonable gun-control legislation from being enacted.

The extreme left has not, at least until recently, exhibited comparable power. This may now be changing with the growing influence of the hard-left within the Democratic Party, and especially among young people. At the moment, hard-left extremists do not have the power to implement those aspects of their agenda that are strongly opposed by liberal centrists within the party. For example, Sanders's supporters would not succeed in getting Congress—even had Sanders been elected President—to approve single-payer health insurance for all if it required union members, teachers, and others to give up their current insurance. Nor are they likely to get the Democratic Party to include in its platform support for the boycott movement against Israel (BDS) or other overtly anti-Israel measures. But they may soon have the power to prevent the passing and implementation of centrist liberal programs with which they disagree, such as requiring federally funded universities to assure due process for students accused of sexual misconduct or speech deemed offensive by some groups. It remains to be seen whether they have the power to block aid to Israel, or to condition it on Israel bending to their will. They will surely try.

It is in the nature of our Constitution's structural constraints that they generally deny extremists the power to *enact* and/or *implement* their radical and/or reactionary policies, but they sometimes give them the power to *stop* or *slow down* centrist policies approved by the centrist majority. The result is often frustrating gridlock, which the Framers apparently viewed as preferable to efficient extremism. Our Constitution was not designed to "make the trains run on time."

Our enduring Constitution has done a commendable job in protecting the liberty of Americans from the extremes of Fascism, Communism, and other dangerous "isms" that have plagued other nations. But, as the great jurist Learned Hand warned: "Liberty lies in the hearts of men and women; when it dies there, no constitution, no law, no court can save it; no constitution, no law, no court can even do much to help it." We have seen liberty die in many parts of the world during many periods of history. It has died in nations with constitutions that provided strong theoretical protections against tyranny. But these parchment proclamations did little to preserve the rule of law when the people were prepared, in the words of Benjamin Franklin, to "give up essential liberty" for the safety, security, and efficiency that dictators promise.

Fortunately, our centrist Constitution, with its cumbersome checks and balances against efficient extremism, is a *reflection* of the character of most Americans, in whose hearts liberty lives. So our *combination* of *external* constitutional safeguards and our *internal* love of liberty will, hopefully, provide strong barriers against the false promises of extremists who would sacrifice liberty for efficiency in achieving their ideologically pure goals. In this respect, Judge Hand may have overstated it when he said that no constitution "can even do much to help it." During times of crisis, when some were inclined to exchange liberty for security, our Constitution did sometimes, but not always, "help" to preserve our fundamental rights. During McCarthyism, the courts slowed down the move toward repression; during the Civil Rights Movement, the courts helped end segregation. But when a liberal president, FDR, ordered American citizens of Japanese descent to be confined in detention centers, the Supreme Court legitimated—to its everlasting shame—that denial of basic liberties.

With its "inefficient" mechanisms of governance—especially its checks and balances against any branch or office holder assuming too much power—the Constitution has slowed down the march toward authoritarianism, but in the end, it was the citizens who have cast their votes in favor of centrism and against extremism, because the centrism of our constitutional structure well suits the American character and our love of liberty. Whether these elements will be enough to protect our liberties from the threats posed by extremism remains to be seen. One of the most fundamental safeguards designed by the Framers was a vibrant, free, and independent press. But, as we shall see in the coming chapter, much of the media has used its constitutional right of free expression to promote and foster the divisiveness and extremism that our constitutional structure was designed to prevent.

CHAPTER 7

The Death of the Centrist Non-Partisan Media: Cause or Effect?

Walter Cronkite could not get a job on television today. He personified the centrist, neutral media that no longer exists. Viewers trusted his reporting, believed the information he conveyed, and had no idea whether his personal politics were left or right. So when he came out against the Vietnam War, near the end of his career, it had a profound impact on public opinion. I got to know Walter after he retired and spent time on Martha's Vineyard with his beloved boat *Wyntje*. It was only at that point that I learned of his liberal leanings. Having watched him for years on television, I had no idea how strongly he felt about the issues he objectively reported.

There are no Walter Cronkites on television today, especially not on cable TV, which dominates the airwaves 24/7. Nor are there any Walter Cronkites on talk radio, which is often more extreme in its partisanship.

No one can know for certain whether the partisan bias of today's media is a cause or effect of the growing divide among Americans. The media today operates in silos. They make more money appealing to a niche audience and telling them what they want to hear than they would if they were to report the news objectively. Too many viewers simply don't want to be exposed to any information that is inconsistent with their preconceived narrative. They crave "comfort" media, which feeds them comforting news and doesn't make them challenge or rethink their preconceptions. They want to nod their heads in agreement when they are given "facts," and they want to smile or smirk when "their" commentators put down their enemies. The last thing they want are inconvenient truths—news that makes them wonder if they may be wrong. They disdain cognitive dissonance in a world dominated by actual dissonance, contradiction, and confusion. They have become intellectually lazy because they are so certain of the correctness of their partisan positions. They do not believe that those who disagree with them have anything worth hearing. John Stuart Mill warned of a time when "both teachers and learners go to sleep at their post." That time is upon us. Media moguls have learned that partisanship sells soap and other products that generate media profits. They cater to a core audience, a base that agrees with their partisan positions and will buy their advertised wares. In order to maintain that niche audience, the pundits and commentators don't want to risk offending them with facts that disturb their comfort.

Talk radio and cable television have contributed significantly to the current divisiveness, but other factors—most importantly the social media and the movements of both parties away from the center—have made the public receptive to this media divide.

In this chapter, I will describe some of my own experiences over the past half-century, beginning with my role as a centrist liberal legal analyst for the *New York Times*, *The New Republic*, public television and radio, and other centrist liberal media. When cable TV began, I was a regular on Larry King, even serving as a guest host on several occasions, as well as on other CNN shows. Then I became a frequent guest on Anderson Cooper, Piers Morgan, Chris Cuomo, Don Lemon, and other CNN and MSNBC evening shows. I often sparred with my former student Jeffrey Toobin. But when I persisted in arguing that the Democratic efforts to impeach President Trump violated the Constitution, Jeffrey Zucker—the head of CNN—issued an order banning me from appearing on his network as a commentator. I was interviewed on two or three occasions as a newsmaker when I argued in the Senate, but not since then.

I am no longer invited to appear on CNN to offer my constitutional analysis. They are ok with having arch–conservative Republicans, whom they use as "exhibits" to demonstrate the absurdity of their views. But the last thing they want is a genuine liberal Democrat who argues that some of their positions with regard to President Trump are illiberal, anti-Democratic, and inconsistent with the Constitution. Today, although my views haven't changed, I am invited largely by the *Wall Street Journal* and Fox News to offer my centrist liberal positions. I am insufficiently partisan for CNN, MSNBC, and even *The New York Times.* It's a sign of the changing times, and is certainly not limited to me.

Before we get into detail about the current partisanship of the media, let us recall that this is not entirely new to American history. Going back to the iconic acquittal of John Peter Zenger nearly half a century before the establishment of the United States, we have seen bias in the media. Zenger's *New York Weekly Journal* was anything but an objective purveyor of the news, specializing in screeds against the British colonial government. His acquittal was against the law at that time, but the jury engaged in civil disobedience and helped establish a precedent for freedom of the press in the colonies.

Following the establishment of our new republic, politicians used the press to further their partisan interests. Thomas Jefferson was particularly adept at getting friendly writers to issue biased reports against his political opponents. John Adams, when he was elected president in 1796, responded by having Congress enact the Alien and Sedition laws that sought to limit the freedom established by the Zenger trial. Throughout American history—from Andrew Jackson, to Abraham Lincoln, to Ulysses Grant, to Theodore Roosevelt—the partisan press played an important role in shaping American politics, sometimes for the better, often for the worse. Near the turn of the 20th century, John Randolph Hearst introduced a new element. His "yellow press" was more interested in reporting scandal, repeating gossip, enflaming readers, and creating news than it was in objective reporting. It is claimed by some historians that his yellow press—along with that of his arch competitor Joseph Pulitzer—contributed to America's decision to go to war against Spain in 1898.

Media bias can also take the form of *refusal* to publish important information that is inconsistent with the ideology of the publisher. The most notorious example of such bias was the under-reporting by the *New York Times* of the Holocaust while it was occurring and known to its reporters. Its publisher, Arthur Hays Sulzberger, was a German Jew who did not want his paper to be "too Jewish." So he relegated news about the mass-murder of Europe's Jews to the back pages, alongside "the soap and shoe polish ads."[84] Between 1939 and 1945, reports of what is now called the Holocaust only rarely appeared on the front page, and even more rarely identified the victims as Jews.[85]

In recent years, the nature of the bias has changed somewhat, reflecting and influencing the current political divisiveness of our nation. The central figure is President Donald Trump. We have had divisive presidents in the past, whom people either loved or hated–Abraham Lincoln, Franklin Delano Roosevelt, and Barack Obama come to mind. But we have never before experienced the kind of unforgiving divide that now surrounds the presidency of Donald Trump. When it comes to Trump, everyone is forced to choose a side: either he is the worst president in history, who has done nothing good, or he is the greatest president, who has done nothing wrong. There is little room for calibrated assessment, for nuance, for "on the one hand," "on the other hand," balance. We must all pick a team and stick with them, as much of the media have done.

I have refused to play that game. I remain a liberal Democrat who voted for Hillary Clinton and for every Democratic presidential candidate before her. I voted for Joe Biden in the 2020 Democratic primary. I am critical of many, perhaps even most, of President Trump's policies, especially with regard to immigration, taxation, gun control, the environment, the Coronavirus, voting by mail, and healthcare. I support some of his policies with regard to combatting terrorism, making NATO share the economic burden of dealing with Russia, criminal justice reform, recognition of Jerusalem and Golan Heights, the proposed Peace Plan, and his executive order cutting federal funding to universities that fail to combat bigotry against Jews and their nation

84 Ari Goldman, "In Denial." *Columbia Magazine*, Spring 2005.

85 Laurel Left, *Buried by the Times* (Cambridge University Press, 2005), pp. 2-3.

state. I did not approve of his handling of the Ukrainian matter, but I did not believe he committed a constitutionally impeachable offense.

In other words, I am not on either team. I call them as I see them. I defend the Constitution and the law, not parties or presidents. That's what liberals do. This atypical posture confuses media bookers, viewers, and listeners, who demand to know which side I'm on—am I *for* Trump or *against* him? The pro-Trump zealots are unhappy that I remain a liberal Democrat who opposes many of Trump's policies. The anti-Trump extremists (and even some non-extremists) are furious at me for offering an interpretation of the Constitution that precludes President Trump's impeachments on the grounds voted by the House. They fail to understand (or pretend not to understand) how anybody who isn't on Trump's *side* can oppose his impeachment. So many people confronted me with this "contradiction," that my wife finally had a T-shirt printed with my answer: "It's The Constitution, Stupid!"

Matters came to a head when I agreed to argue in the Senate in opposition to President Trump's removal.[86] My argument centered on the history and meaning of the constitutional criteria: "treason, bribery or other high crimes and misdemeanors." Since "misdemeanors" were a species of crimes—in the words of the 18th century commentator, William Blackstone, "synonymous" with crime—the *plain meaning* of the criteria is that it requires criminal-like behavior akin to treason and bribery. It does not include "abuse of power" or "obstruction of Congress"—the two charges brought against Trump by the House. The Framers expressly rejected similarly open-ended criteria, such as "maladministration," for fear—in James Madison's words—that "so vague a term will be an equivalent to tenure during pleasure of the Senate." The terms "abuse" and "obstruction" are at least as vague and subject to abuse by Congress, as evidenced by the historical reality that most of our presidents have been accused by their opponents of abusing their power, and many of obstructive behavior. So I argued that the House charges themselves—"abuse of power" and "obstruction of Congress"—were not constitutionally permissible criteria for impeachment, and

86 A Senate official told me that at eighty-one, I was the oldest lawyer to argue a presidential impeachment and removal case to the Senate.

that no amount of evidence or no new witnesses could change that constitutional barrier to removal.[87] But I made it absolutely clear that if a president were to be charged with criminal-like behavior, such as extortion, perjury, or other comparable crimes and misdemeanors, he could be impeached. I emphasized that no one—not the President *nor Congress*—is above the law.

My argument apparently had an impact on Senators, especially regarding the need to call witnesses. *The Washington Post* described it as, "The most favored speech for quoting among GOP Senators. It provided them cover, should they need it, for refusing to allow witnesses in the trial of Trump, for voting to acquit him and, in the event damaging evidence emerges after the trial, for slamming it as irrelevant." According to Senator Ted Cruz: "Dershowitz's learned insight played a critical role convincing Senators that the President's conduct did not rise to the constitutional threshold of "other high crimes and misdemeanors." Senator Jim Inhofe said he "agree[d] with Alan Dershowitz—a liberal Democrat—who explained so well that more witnesses won't change the fact that President Trump did not commit an impeachable offense." Several other Senators came up to me after my presentation to tell me how persuasive I had been. This worried the Democratic Impeachment Managers and their senate allies, so they worked in tandem with CNN in an effort to discredit me and my arguments. The story of how CNN worked hand-in-hand with the Democrats speaks volumes about the partisan role of the media. So here is the well-documented story.

Following my main argument, Senators were allowed to ask questions through the Chief Justice. Among them was the following:

> The Chief Justice: The question is addressed to counsel for the President:
>
> As a matter of law, does it matter if there was a quid pro quo? Is it true that quid pro quos are often used in foreign policy?

---

87 When the charges are unconstitutional, as they were here, additional *evidence* becomes constitutionally irrelevant, unless the charges are amended.

I began my answer by emphasizing what I had already said in my opening argument: namely that "If the quid pro quo were in some way *illegal*," that would be impeachable. I went on to provide examples of illegal and impeachable quid pro quos: if the President sought a "kickback" or some other "personal pecuniary" benefit; or if he had a "corrupt motive." In other words, if a president engaged in criminal, corrupt, or financially self-serving conduct, he *could* be impeached. I also said, that if a president engaged in *completely lawful conduct* that was motivated in part by his desire to be re-elected, that "mixed-motive" would not turn lawful conduct into an impeachable offense. I had earlier provided the following example from President Lincoln, quoting Professor Joshua Blackman:

> In 1864, during the height of the Civil War, President Lincoln encouraged Gen. William Sherman to allow soldiers in the field to return to Indiana to vote. What was Lincoln's primary motivation? He wanted to make sure that the government of Indiana remained in the hands of Republican loyalists who would continue the war until victory. Lincoln's request risked undercutting the military effort by depleting the ranks. Moreover, during this time, soldiers from the remaining states faced greater risks than did the returning Hoosiers. Lincoln had dueling motives. Privately, he sought to secure a victory for his party. But the president, as a party leader and commander-in-chief, made a decision with life-or-death consequences.

Professor Blackman drew the following relevant conclusion from this and other historical events:

> Politicians routinely promote their understanding of the general welfare, while, in the back of their minds, considering how these actions will affect their popularity. Often, the two concepts overlap: what's good for the country is good for the official's re-election. All politicians understand this dynamic.[88]

---

88 The quote is from original arguments. I paraphrased it as follows in my answer to the question:

My point was self-evident and uncontroversial: that a *lawful* act committed by a president would not become an impeachable offense even if it were motivated, in part, by a desire to be re-elected. No reasonable person could disagree with what I really said. So CNN deliberately *doctored* the video of my answer to make it sound like I said that a president could do *anything*—even *commit a serious crime*—if part of his motive was to be reelected. Here is how Paul Begala, a paid CNN commentator, deliberately misdescribed what I said: According to Dershowitz, presidents are "immune from *every criminal act*, so long as they could plausibly claim they did it to boost their re-election effort." CNN Paid commentator Joe Lockhart went even further, claiming that I was giving President Trump a "license to *commit crimes*" and that is what you hear "from Stalin . . . Mussolini, Hitler" when they commit "genocide." Another CNN employee, John Berman, summarized my argument as follows: A "president" seeking re-election "can do *anything—anything*." He correctly characterized such an argument as "somewhere between bizarre and nuts." What he didn't tell his viewers is that I had made exactly *the opposite argument*: namely that a president *cannot* do anything that is in *any way illegal*, corrupt, or self-enriching, regardless of his motive to be re-elected. Berman then played the doctored video, which was deliberately edited by CNN to eliminate all my references to "illegal," "corrupt," or "self-enriching conduct." It was as if I had said the following: "This is what I *don't believe*: A president can do anything illegal as long as his motive was to be re-elected. I don't believe that for a moment," and CNN then edited it to omit the words "This is what I don't believe" and "I don't believe that for a moment," playing *only* the words "A president can do anything illegal as long as his motive

---

I quoted President Lincoln, when President Lincoln told General Sherman to let the troops go to Indiana so they could vote for the Republican Party. Let's assume the President was running at that point and it was in his electoral interests to have the soldiers put at risk the lives of many, many other soldiers who would be left without their company. Would that be an unlawful quid pro quo? No, because the President, A, believed it was in the national interest, but B, he believed that his election was essential to victory in the Civil War. Every president believes that. That is why it is so dangerous to try to psychoanalyze the President, to try to get into the intricacies of the human mind.

was to be re-elected," and attributing these words and ideas to me.[89]

---

89 My entire answer is as follows:

"Mr. Counsel Dershowitz: Mr. Chief Justice, thank you very much for your question.

Yesterday, I had the privilege of attending the rolling-out of a peace plan by the President of the United States regarding the Israel-Palestine conflict, and I offered you a hypothetical the other day: What if a Democratic President were to be elected and Congress were to authorize much money to either Israel or the Palestinians and the Democratic President were to say to Israel 'No; I am going to withhold this money unless you stop all settlement growth' or to the Palestinians 'I will withhold the money Congress authorized to you unless you stop paying terrorists,' and the President said 'Quid pro quo. If you don't do it, you don't get the money'? There is no one in this Chamber who would regard that as in any way unlawful. The only thing that would make a quid pro quo unlawful is if the quo were in some way illegal.

Now, we talked about motive. There are three possible motives that a political figure can have: One, a motive in the public interest, and the Israel argument would be in the public interest; the second is in his own political interest; and the third, which hasn't been mentioned, would be in his own financial interest, just putting money in the bank. I want to focus on the second one just for the moment.

Every public official whom I know believes that his election is in the public interest. Mostly, you are right. Your election is in the public interest. If a President does something he believes will help him get elected □ in the public interest □ that cannot be the kind of quid pro quo that results in impeachment.

I quoted President Lincoln, when President Lincoln told General Sherman to let the troops go to Indiana so that they could vote for the Republican Party. Let's assume the President was running at that point and it was in his electoral interests to have these soldiers put at risk the lives of many, many other soldiers who would be left without their company. Would that be an unlawful quid pro quo? No, because the President, A, believed it was in the national interest, but B, he believed that his own election was essential to victory in the Civil War. Every President believes that. That is why it is so dangerous to try to psychoanalyze the President, to try to get into the intricacies of the human mind.

Everybody has mixed motives, and for there to be a constitutional impeachment based on mixed motives would permit almost any President to be impeached.

How many Presidents have made foreign policy decisions after checking with their political advisers and their pollsters? If you are just acting in the national interest, why do you need pollsters? Why do you need political advisers? Just do what is best for the country. But if you want to balance what is in the public interest with what is in your party's electoral interest and your own electoral interest, it is impossible to discern how much weight is given to one or the other.

Now, we may argue that it is not in the national interest or a particular President to get re-elected or for a particular Senator or member of Congress □ and maybe we are right; it is not in the national interest for everybody who is running to be elected □ but for it to be impeachable, you would have to discern that he or she made a decision solely on the basis of, as the House Managers put it, corrupt motives, and it cannot be a *corrupt motive* if you have a mixed motive that partially

That would be doctoring the video, and what they actually did was functionally no different.

The doctored tape was played over and over again on CNN, and then used by the Democratic senators to discredit me. It didn't work for the senators, who actually heard my entire answer, but it did fool viewers, who only saw the doctored tape.

Some Democratic senators and congressmen who heard what I actually said simply lied about it, relying on the CNN-doctored video. Senator Chuck Schumer called the statement misquoted by CNN, "The Dershowitz Doctrine," which he said would have resulted in President Nixon's acquittal, ignoring the fact that I told the senators, including him, that I *supported* the impeachment and removal of Nixon. Congressman Adam Schiff described the misquoted view attributed to me by CNN as "lawless," despite my insistence that if the President broke the law, he could be impeached. Moreover, what I said about mixed motives applied to *all* elected officials, not only presidents. I discussed all "political figure[s]" and "public official[s]," as several senators noted appreciatively after I made my response. But CNN made it sound as if I were expanding *presidential* power at the expense of other branches.

Not a single CNN commentator tried to correct the record, even though they knew CNN had doctored the recording. Both the *Wall*

---

involves the national interest, partially involves electoral, and *does not involve personal pecuniary interest.*

The House Managers do not allege that this decision, this quid pro quo, as they call it – and the question is based on the hypothesis there was a quid pro quo. I am not attacking the facts. *They never allege that it was based on pure financial reasons. It would be a much harder case.* If a hypothetical President of the United States said to a hypothetical leader of a foreign country: unless you build a hotel with my name on it and unless you give me *a million-dollar kickback*, I will withhold the funds. *That is an easy case. That is purely corrupt and in the purely private interest.*

But a complex middle case is: I want to be elected. I think I am a great President. I think I am the greatest President there ever was, and if I am not elected, the national interest will suffer greatly. That cannot be. (Emphasis added.)

The Chief Justice. Thank you counsel.

Mr. Dershowitz. Thank you Mr. Chief Justice."

No honest person could read that answer as saying or suggesting that a president could do "anything," even commit crimes, in order to be re-elected.

Street Journal and *The New York Times* reported my answer correctly. The *WSJ* reported:

> The media claim[s] that defense lawyer Alan Dershowitz said a President can do anything to further is re-election as long as he thinks it is in the national interest. This isn't what he said. The Harvard professor said explicitly that a President can be impeached for criminal acts.

The Times reported on my position as follows:

> Some Democratic senators and other critics accused him of suggesting that even Nixon was not impeachable, despite his clear crimes. But that accusation is incompatible with Mr. Dershowitz's main argument: that an impeachable "high crime and misdemeanor" requires an indictable offense.

But CNN persisted in its deliberate misreporting.

What CNN did was not accidental, or even negligent. It was a deliberate decision made at the highest levels of the network to doctor the recording explicitly to change the meaning of what I said. I know this for a fact. And they have not denied it because they know I have the evidence. That is why I am considering suing CNN for malicious defamation.

I am a lifelong defender of a broad view of the First Amendment, having been a law clerk when *NY Times v. Sullivan* was decided, and having argued freedom of speech cases in numerous courts, including the Supreme Court. I believe that the media has what I have called, "the right to be wrong," as long as their "mistake" is honest, rather than malicious. But what CNN did was not a "mistake." It was a calculated, malicious decision, made with premeditation and explicit knowledge of its falsity for the express purpose of attacking my credibility. In a 1991 decision in which *The New Yorker* was sued for defamation, the Supreme Court ruled that the First Amendment did not protect "deliberate alteration of the words uttered by a plaintiff," if "the alteration results in a material change in the meaning conveyed by the statement." That is what occurred when CNN deliberately edited the recording to materially change my meaning.

Moreover, CNN has refused to correct the record, going so far as to cancel a scheduled appearance by me in which I was planning to tell viewers what I had actually said. I had accepted an invitation to appear on the "Smerconish" show. The car was arranged. I was supposed to be at the top of the show. Then the order came down from on high: "Cancel Dershowitz, because he criticized our coverage of what he said." At first CNN denied I was cancelled for my criticism, claiming it was just a change in programming, but eventually several people at the network confided the truth to me: you can't criticize "our bosses" and expect to be on our network. So much for the marketplace of ideas on CNN. So much for freedom of speech. So much for self-criticism or admitting their mistakes. Instead we have lies, cover-ups and lies about the cover-ups. The public, including CNN viewers, are not generally aware of the lack of journalistic standards at CNN. For CNN, the partisan ends justify any means.

My story is only one of many that demonstrated the bias of the media and the decision of networks, especially but not exclusively the cable networks, to take sides and help their "team" by what they report, what they refuse to report, and how they report. My story is, tragically, representative of the growing ideological and partisan divide among networks, reporters, and viewers.

The media often reminds us of Jefferson's famous remark, made *before* he was elected president, that "were it left to me to decide whether we should have a government without newspapers or newspapers without a government, I should not hesitate a moment to prefer the latter." But they never quote what he said *after* he was president and victimized by the partisan press: "The man who reads nothing at all is better educated than the man who reads nothing but newspapers." I would paraphrase that by adding much of cable TV and talk radio. Today's partisan media is not a solution to the nation's divisiveness, it *is* the problem.

CHAPTER 8

Liberalism in a Time of Pandemic

Times of crisis test the limits of any philosophy of governance. Liberalism is no exception. For it to be a compelling theory, it must be able to deal in real terms and real time with exigent circumstances. As Thomas Payne put it two and a half centuries ago, during the dark days of the American Revolution: "These are the times that try men's souls." Emergencies also try the limits of civil liberties. It is a cliché that the first casualty of war is often liberty, but that is also true of other emergencies as well. In this chapter, I will explore the way in which the United States has dealt with civil liberties during prior crises, as well as during the current pandemic emergency. I will then suggest what I believe is the appropriate liberal approach to these recurring, if infrequent, situations.

Half a century ago, I published a series of articles about civil liberties during times of national emergency, and I offered a liberal perspective on how our nation, and especially its courts, have responded to past crises and how they should respond to future emergencies.[90] Our record as a nation in times of crises is decidedly mixed. The big picture is positive: we have never succumbed to the false prophets of Fascism, Communism or other forms of long-term authoritarian

90 Dershowitz, *Shouting Fire* pp. 415-483.

rule, as many currently democratic nations—such as Germany, Italy, Spain, Argentina, and Chile—have done. But on a smaller level, we have allowed massive violations of civil liberties, especially during wartime. And some of these violations were engineered by our most liberal presidents: Lincoln suspended the writ of habeas corpus; Wilson authorized the Palmer Raids; Roosevelt detained more than 100,000 Japanese-Americans during World War II. Other presidents and governors have declared martial law, which is a contradiction in terms, because if it is "martial"—that is, "the will of the generals," as Lord Wellington characterized it—it is not "law."

After reviewing our mixed history, I speculated on what we "could reasonably expect" from courts if any American president during a period of dire emergency were once again to suspend important constitutional safeguards. Here is what I wrote back in 1971:

> Our past experiences suggest the following outline: the courts— especially the Supreme Court—will generally not interfere with the executive's handling of a genuine emergency while it still exists. They will employ every technique of judicial avoidance at their disposal to postpone decision until the crisis has passed. The likely exceptions to this rule of judicial postponement will be cases of clear abuse where no real emergency can be said to exist, and cases in which delay would result in irrevocable loss of rights, such as those involving the death penalty. Once the emergency has passed, the courts will generally not approve further punishment; they will order the release of all those sentenced to imprisonment or death in violation of ordinary constitutional safeguards. But they will not entertain damage suits for illegal confinement ordered during the course of the emergency.[91]

Since I wrote those words, we have experienced the terrorist attacks of 9/11, after which Congress passed and presidents enforced draconian measures, with mixed reactions from the courts. These measures were directed largely against Muslims, as the Roosevelt detention order was

91 Dershowitz, *Shouting Fire*, pp. 417 - 419.

directed against Americans of Japanese descent. Americans are more likely to accept deprivations of civil liberties when they target "the other," in order to protect "us." Of course, in both of those situations, at least some of "the others" were "us," but that is not necessarily the perception during times of crisis.

The current Coronavirus pandemic threatens the entire world, and yet there has been demonization and finger-pointing against the Chinese and Asian Americans, as well as some religious groups. Fear begets stereotyping and bigotry, as well as a willingness by some to sacrifice too much liberty for safety. Among others, it promotes extremism and efforts to exploit the crisis for ideological and/or partisan advantage. As Rahm Emanuel, President Obama's Chief of Staff, put it: "You never want a serious crisis to go to waste." He explained that a crisis "is an opportunity to do things that you think you could not do before." Emanuel's quote has been widely circulated during the Coronavirus crisis by *both* sides, demonstrating that it is clearly a double-edged sword. Extremists often exploit crises to frighten or bully citizens into accepting governmental actions that they would not accept during normal times. For example, anti-abortion extremists have tried to use the pandemic as an excuse to shut down clinics. Gun control advocates have used it to try to limit gun sales. There are other examples as well that will be discussed in the coming pages. The important point is that times of crisis require the attributes of liberalism: renewed commitment to the rule of law; striking appropriate balances among liberty, privacy, and safety; skepticism about "truths," whether religious, scientific, or political; concern for the most vulnerable; the need to preserve democratic accountability; and other transcendent values that are too easily marginalized during emergencies. That is why, as soon as it became apparent that we were experiencing a pandemic, I began to write and comment about these issues from my liberal perspective. A liberal, if he or she is to remain true to the philosophy of liberalism, must engage during times of crisis. In the words of Justice Oliver Wendell Holmes Jr., who fought in the Civil War, "Not to have participated in the actions and passions of one's time is to be judged not to have lived."

My first article[92] was entitled, "Coronavirus Raises Legal Issues of Public Safety [and] Personal Liberty." I quoted Justice Holmes's pithy comment that "hard cases make bad law" and warned that hard problems like the Coronavirus challenge our legal system to its core, especially since it is unfolding on "uncharted legal terrain." I then set out the areas in which legal controversies may be played out, the first of which is the right of citizens not to be confined to their homes for long periods of time. I predicted that most Americans would comply voluntarily, but some will resist, as some resist mandatory vaccinations, despite their proven necessity to prevent the spread of contagious diseases:

> The law will give officials authority to compel compliance and to punish noncompliance, but it may not have the resources to act effectively. We lack sufficiently trained personnel to safely enforce all preventative measures. We may have to employ deterrence, or the threat of harsh punishment for those who fail to comply. This too is an imperfect solution to a crisis that is not amenable to perfect solutions. We need to aim for the best, or least-worst, approaches to provide the most practical preventive measures.

I then articulated the centrist liberal position:

> If compromises with liberty are required in our country by the exigencies of the current crisis, it is imperative that these compromises be narrowly tailored to the needs of the day and be limited in duration. Our legal and political systems are being tested. In order to pass these tests, our nation and the world need goodwill, sacrifice, wisdom, and compromise, attributes that are in short supply during this age of divisiveness, recrimination, and extremism. We must rise above these differences to confront this dangerous virus that now threatens us all.

---

92 Alan Dershowitz, "Coronavirus Raises Legal Issue of Public Safety or Personal Liberty," *The Hill*, March 11, 2020.

Several days later, I wrote a controversial article challenging the medical advice we were getting from official public health sources. It was entitled "Believe Science, But Be Skeptical of Scientists." I began by disclosing my liberal trait of being a skeptic by nature—never believing what I read or hear without evidence. I then applied that skepticism to two "truths" being promoted by public health scientists: first, that "face masks don't work;" and second, that "the virus is only contagious by physical contact with infected individuals or surfaces which they touched," but *not* "by airborne or aerosol transmission."

I challenged the facemask advice:

> The officials also said that if individuals buy facemasks in large numbers, there won't be enough for health providers. That I believe. But the combination of reasons—they don't work, but they are important for health providers—immediately set off alarm bells in my skeptical mind. If they don't work for ordinary individuals, why should they work for health providers? Maybe there is a relevant difference. I keep an open but skeptical mind, while wearing the mask that I bought just in case.

I also challenged the claim that the virus could not travel through the air:

> I was skeptical of this claim because it seemed inconsistent with the speed and frequency with which transmissions were occurring around the world. I told my friends and family to act as if they could get the virus through the air. There is no downside to being more careful.

We now know, as the result of extensive research and experience, that both of those "scientific" claims were wrong, or at least exaggerated, but at the time I wrote, they were taken as gospel. For liberals, there is no scientific "gospel," only a never-ending search for ever-changing truths.

I ended my article with a description of a cartoon that showed a typical guy looking at his computer screen and saying: "That's odd: my

Facebook friends who were constitutional scholars just a month ago are now infectious disease experts." Be skeptical of armchair "experts."

A subsequent article dealt with the rights of prisoners, who are particularly sensitive to the virus:

> A prison sentence, or the denial of bail, are not supposed to be sentences of death or disease. Steps should be taken now to reduce the risk not only to prisoners but to those who come in contact with them in prison or upon release. Among these preventative steps should be the following: allowing elderly non-violent prisoners who are near the end of their sentences to be sent home; those who still have considerable time to serve should be temporarily furloughed to home confinement, subject to increased punishment if they violate the strict conditions of the furlough; pre-trial and pre-appeal defendants should be allowed to remain at home unless they pose a threat of violence; imprisonment of sentenced non-violent defendants should be deferred from month to month as we monitor the spread of the virus; summonses should replace arrests in most non-violent cases; fines and other non-custodial punishments should be more widely imposed as long as custody poses life-threatening risks; other creative amelioratives should be considered.[93]

Not content merely to write on behalf of vulnerable prisoners, I helped litigate on their behalf as well, resulting in some being sent home under house arrest for the duration of the crisis. That, too, is what liberals do. We act as best we can to effectuate our liberal policies. Some of the steps I advocated are ones which, as a liberal, I would have liked to see taken even in the absence of a pandemic, but the need to take them has increased with the unique threats to prisoners and guards. This is quite different from how some right-wing extremists are trying to exploit the pandemic to push programs that bear no reasonable relationship to the problem at hand, such as banning pornography

---

93 Alan Dershowitz, "The Prisoner Dilemma in the Age of Coronavirus," Gatestone Institute, March 17, 2020, https://www.gatestoneinstitute.org/15753/coronavirus-prisoners.

and abortion. I wrote an article entitled, "Exploiting Pandemic for Ideological Advantage is Wrong."[94] I quoted an anti-porn website, which compared the porn "pandemic" to Coronavirus:

> Like the Coronavirus, pornography use is silent but deadly, a powerful disease that has had devastating effects across our society. Although Coronavirus may attract more headlines today, pornography will be with us for the long haul. Porn cannot be vaccinated against. It has a nearly $100 billion industry devoted to its spread worldwide and few are brave enough to stand against it.

The anti-porn zealots were outraged by the decision of some porn sites to make their products free for shut-ins in order to encourage what they euphemistically called "home remedies" to the sexual deprivations resulting from quarantine. The porn sites even showed actors "wearing protective masks." This didn't stop the zealots from arguing that, "As bad as Coronavirus is, we cannot afford to fight one disease by simply trading it for another. Now more than ever, we must join together to take on the pornography industry and defeat the terrible porn *epidemic*." (Emphasis added). I responded that, "Now more than ever, we must not dilute additional resources to unnecessarily constraining basic liberties that are unrelated to the public health needs to prevent the spread of the Coronavirus."

These anti-porn crusaders have a First Amendment right to advocate their anti-liberal views, but the anti-abortion extremists have no constitutional right to shut down abortion clinics, as I argued in my article, which cited the CEO of the Center for Reproductive Rights: "It is very clear that anti-abortion rights politicians are shamelessly exploiting this crisis to achieve what has been their long-standing ideological goal: to ban abortion in the United States." To prove that point, she cited efforts by some states to ban abortion *pills* as well as other methods of ending a pregnancy that do not require hospitalization or clinics. She also pointed out that banning abortion is far more

94 Dershowitz, "Exploiting Pandemic for Ideological Advantage is Wrong." [Full Cite p. 23]

dangerous to public health because it will force women to travel long distances, citing a study that women seeking abortions during this pandemic would have to travel up to twenty times further than normal if some states shut down local clinics.

I wrote about one difficult issue that hit close to home. Harvard send out a letter to all faculty and students insisting that it is of "paramount" importance that the identities of those members of the Harvard community who test positive be kept confidential: "The last thing they need, or any of us would want for them, is public attention and scrutiny." As a liberal, I certainly support the rights of medical privacy, but in an op-ed about the Harvard directive, I suggested that the benefits of confidentiality should be balanced against its costs in the context of a pandemic:

> If the names are not disclosed, other individuals who may have come in contact with the carrier but have not been notified may be denied information that might cause them to be tested or quarantined, increasing the threat of spreading the virus. Compelled nondisclosure, moreover, also sends a message that there may be a stigma attached to being known as a carrier. That may again deter testing.[95]

I cited the benefits resulting from Tom Hanks' decision to go public:

> Actor Tom Hanks performed a public service when he announced that he had tested positive for the Coronavirus. I recently learned that someone I know had himself tested after learning that the wife of Hanks, with whom he had been in contact, had also tested positive. Others have also been tested after learning the names of people with whom they have been in contact who tested positive.

I acknowledged that Hanks is a public figure, and not every afflicted person will want their condition made known. I then provided my own conclusion, based on a liberal balancing test:

---

95 Alan Dershowitz, "Is There a Right to Anonymity for Coronavirus Carriers in America?" *The Hill*, March 18, 2020.

> As a member of the Harvard community, I will continue to abide by the guidance of our leaders, while encouraging debate about this difficult issue. My own tentative view, which is subject to being influenced by persuasive arguments and data to the contrary, is that patients who tests positive should be encouraged to follow Hanks and disclose their names or allow their names to be disclosed by health officials, if necessary to alert others. If they refuse, these officials should have the discretion to overrule when there are compelling public health reasons. Indeed, the issue of anonymity is a good place to start a general discussion about how to strike the proper civil liberties balance in times of crisis.

The single most important question facing all democracies at a time of pandemic is what would happen if the public health situation became so severe that scheduled elections could not be held. That question becomes even more important if there are suspicions that one political party would benefit from elections being cancelled or postponed. So I wrote two op-eds setting out a liberal approach to these issues.

There is no acceptable reason for an election to be cancelled, since there are alternatives to live voting on a single day. But it is possible, though unlikely, that voting by mail might become unrealistic if the pandemic were to become so much worse that it endangered the lives of postal workers.

This has never happened before, and it probably won't happen this year, but law professors specialize in assessing hypothetical scenarios, so I provided my assessment from a liberal perspective.

Any assessment must begin with the words of the Constitution, which, however, provide no definitive answer. But they do provide some clear conclusions. First and foremost, absent an election, the incumbent president does *not* continue to serve in an interim capacity until an election is held. Unlike parliamentary democracies such as Israel, where Prime Minister Benjamin Netanyahu continued to serve until an agreement was reached, our president's term ends on a date specific, regardless of whether or not a successor has been picked.

The 20th amendment is unambiguous: "The terms of the President and Vice President *shall* end at noon on 20 January. . ." (Emphasis added). Nothing could seem clearer. The end of that paragraph provides that "the terms of their successors shall then begin." But what if no successors have been elected?

Does the president then continue to serve as an interim office holder? The constitutional answer is no, because his or her "term" definitely ends at noon on the twentieth of January. If not re-elected, he becomes a private citizen on that day. Who, then, serves as president? The Constitution itself provides no clear answer. Unlike when a president is impeached or dies, there is no clear succession plan in place for a situation in which there has been no voting.

The 20th amendment does speak to the issue of what happens if neither a president nor a vice president shall have been chosen "before the time fixed for the beginning of his term," but it refers to a somewhat different scenario:

> Congress may by law provide for the case wherein neither a President *elect* nor a Vice President *elect* shall have qualified, declaring who shall then act as President, or the manner in which one who is to act shall be selected, and such person shall act accordingly, until a President or Vice President shall have qualified. (Emphasis added).

But if there is no election, there is no President or Vice President elect. Congress has provided for a line of succession "if by reason of death, resignation, removal from office, and inability or failure to qualify," there is "neither a President nor Vice President." Again, this does not seem to encompass the absence of an election. There is an obvious gap in our Constitution, because the Framers didn't contemplate a no-election possibility. But even if Congress has the authority to fill the constitutional gap, it isn't clear how they would do it under the current succession law, because the line of succession begins with the Speaker of the House.

But there would be no Speaker if there were no election, because there would be no House, all of whose members would be up for election in November. The terms of all members of the House would end, according to the Constitution, on the third of January. There would be a Senate, with two-thirds of its members who were not up for election still serving.

This is important, because the next in line for the presidency would be the president *pro tempore* of the Senate, who is currently Republican Senator Charles Grassley. But if there were no election, there might be a Democratic majority among the remaining two-thirds of the Senators who were not up for re-election. (unless governors or state legislatures were allowed to fill vacant Senate seats—another uncertainty.) Traditionally, the longest serving majority Senator is given the honor of serving as president *pro tem*. Currently, that is Democratic Senator Patrick Leahy of Vermont. But the Democratic majority could elect any sitting Senator to that role, including Senators Amy Klobuchar, Elizabeth Warren—or even Bernie Sanders. If the succession statute covers a non-election, which itself is doubtful, the Democratic Senator selected to serve as president *pro tem* would become the next president. This uncertainty should be frightening enough to either party to discourage them from trying to cancel the 2020 election.

The alternatives to an election are unthinkable in a democracy: a nation with no president and working legislature; or an interim president not clearly authorized by law.

Because of the utter uncertainty of any alternative to an election, it is in the interest of both parties and all Americans to make sure that the 2020 election is held in a timely, fair, and safe manner.

That is why I wrote another op-ed calling for the immediate appointment by Congress of a blue-ribbon, nonpartisan, credible, and respected commission to explore the options:

> The commission could be chaired by a former Supreme Court justice, such as David Souter. The other members could include former federal and state judges, presidents of universities, and experts in voting. The key for this is credibility. The commission must be seen as, and must actually be, totally nonpartisan. Its only goal is to see that a fair election is conducted this fall with as many people voting and with as little fraud as possible. Options could include voting by mail, by phone, by electronic means, or in person for locations where that could be feasible. The votes need not be cast on a single

> day. . . . There should be safeguards against fraud, such as requiring a mail-in ballot from those who vote electronically so that, if there is a claim that an electronic vote is fraudulent, then it could be checked against the mailed ballot.[96]

I acknowledged the difficulty of finding such a non-partisan group of statesmen and -women in our age of extreme partisan divisiveness. But the alternative is to do nothing and simply hope for the best. That is not the liberal way. We must plan for the worst and assure that, whatever the public health situation turns out to be, the election of November 2020 will be held in the fairest way possible.

Finally, I wrote about the right to protest—safely—which is guaranteed by our First Amendment. So is the right peaceably to assemble and petition the government. But governments have always had the power to impose time, place, and manner restrictions on these important rights. No one has the right to have loudspeakers wake up neighbors in the middle of the night, or to break into legislative assemblies to present their petitions, or to assemble on private property or in a manner that blocks entrance to public buildings.

Against this constitutional background, the question arises whether citizens protesting the current restrictions on movement have the constitutional right to assemble in violation of social distancing rules. They certainly have the right to petition in social media and in other ways that don't endanger public health. But do they have the right to gather together in large crowds to express their views? The constitutional answer depends on several factors.

The first is whether the rules requiring social distancing are actually enforceable by law. Governors and presidents generally have no authority to *make* laws. Only legislatures may make laws that are enforceable through arrest and prosecution. Under certain circumstances, legislatures may delegate the authority to make enforceable rules to the Executive branch—to the president, governors, or mayors—but such delegation must be express and specific. Executives have no inherent

---

96 Alan Dershowitz, "How to Save the 2020 Election," *The Hill*, April 09, 2020, https://thehill.com/opinion/campaign/491967-how-to-save-the-2020-election#.

power to create restrictions on liberty, absent legislative authorization. Executives generally *enforce* the laws *enacted* by legislatures.

Some of the current Executive Orders restricting liberty are of questionable validity absent legislative authorization. That doesn't mean they shouldn't be obeyed, but it does mean that if they are disobeyed, it may be difficult to enforce them through the mechanism of criminal punishment.

If the shutdowns remain in place for a considerable period of time, legislation may be required to authorize long-term restrictions on freedom.

So the first question regarding the recent protests in Wisconsin and elsewhere is whether the protesters were actually violating any enforceable criminal laws or merely disregarding unenforceable Executive Orders. That is generally a question of local law that must be answered before we get to the First Amendment.

Only if the rules prohibiting the gathering of protesters are legally enforceable under state law do we reach the next question of whether these rules violate the First Amendment. And that may depend on how broad the rules are. If they are narrowly tailored to the current public health emergency, they will probably pass muster under the First Amendment. But if they are vague, open ended, and not limited in time, they may well be found to violate the Constitution.

As several Supreme Court Justices have put it: "The Constitution is not a suicide pact." It must be flexible enough to assure that during real emergencies, the government must have the authority, in Jefferson's words, "Of self-preservation, of saving our country when in danger." But the Constitution must also serve as a barrier against government's exploiting emergencies to expand their powers beyond the real needs of the moment. We are seeing that happening in Hungary, Poland, Turkey, and other authoritarian regimes. It must not be allowed to happen here.

The courts, especially the Supreme Court, are the institutions that have been authorized to strike this delicate balance. In general, they have struck it in favor of emergency powers during public health crises, so long as these powers are narrowly drawn, reasonably exercised, and limited in time.

Consider, for example, the closing of churches. It may be reasonable to prevent large crowds from gathering in closed buildings to pray, but it may not be reasonable to prevent churchgoers from sitting in their closed automobiles and listening to a sermon in a drive-in theater that has been converted into a temporary church. Or consider protests by people driving cars in front of government buildings and honking their horns (during the day) or flying U.S. flags upside down.

These types of accommodations may be required by the First Amendment, even during real public-health emergencies, if these actions do not pose realistic dangers of spreading the virus.

Putting aside the legal and constitutional issues, good citizens should comply with reasonable measures designed by responsible officials to prevent or control the spread of a highly contagious, often deadly, virus. Just because there is a right to protest does not mean that it is necessarily right to fully exercise that right, when to do so may endanger your neighbors, family, and strangers. An example in point: protestors may have the right to yell and insult health workers, but doing so is wrong. So I urged my readers to do the right thing, even if they have the right to do the wrong thing.

What I wrote back in 1971 about national emergencies is equally applicable to current crises:

> Liberty, like life itself, needs many sources of nutriment to sustain it. It is not a commodity that can be obtained once and for all and then passively held on to. The difficult struggle for liberty must be endured by every new generation and in each new crisis. What Thomas Paine taught us on the eve of our own Revolution remains true today: "Those who expect to reap the blessings of freedom must, like men [and women] undergo the fatigue of supporting it."

Centrist liberalism provides the best approach to preserving liberty during periods of crises. It is not perfect, but, like democracy itself, it is better than any other approach.

CONCLUSION

The Talmud tells us that the ability to prophesy has ended: "From the day that the Temple was destroyed, prophecy was taken from the prophets and given to the fools." Yogi Berra put it more succinctly: "It's tough to make predictions, especially about the future." Anyone who still believes that polls can predict elections has forgotten November 2016. Even more difficult than predicting the outcome of an election is predicting long-term or even medium-term trends. Who could have foreseen the movement toward right- and left-wing extremism in our politics after the election of such moderates as George H.W. Bush and Bill Clinton, and even the slightly more conservative George W. Bush and slightly more liberal Barack Obama? Who would have guessed that a seventy-eight-year-old Jewish Socialist from Vermont would be the second most popular democratic candidate for president—and the most popular among young Democrats? Who would have predicted 9/11 and our attack on Iraq? Who could have anticipated the Coronavirus pandemic and its cataclysmic impact on our world?

Yet despite these difficulties, it is essential to anticipate the future, especially for anyone who seeks to impact it. The great jurist Oliver Wendell Holmes Jr. wrote that the object of his studies was "prediction"—in his case "the prediction of the incidence of the public force through the instrumentality of the courts." He defined law as, "the prophecies of what the courts will do in fact." As a lawyer, teacher, and writer for nearly sixty years, I have been in the business of anticipating future developments. I advise clients not on what the law *was* or even *is*, but rather what it *will* be when their case comes to be decided. I tried to prepare my students to practice law in the decades *after* their graduation. My books and op-eds have had the immodest goal of having some impact on *future* developments. So with the cautions of the Talmud and Yogi Berra in mind, I will end this book with my assessment of whether the current dangerous trends away from the center and toward malignant left and right-wing extremism are likely to abate, persist, or accelerate. I will try not to let my own strong preference for abatement influence my predictions.

Logic points to acceleration, because the movement away from centrist liberalism and toward the hard-left has been largely fueled by young people, who will soon take over the reins of leadership in politics, the media, academia, business, technology, and other important aspects of American, and indeed international, life. As the British intellectual Tom Mann put it: "The future of the world belongs to the youth of the world, and it is from the youth and not from the old that the fire of life will warm and enlighten the world." It would be logical to assume therefore that current trends toward extremism will only accelerate as the youth assume leadership roles. But what Oliver Wendell Holmes said about law—"The life of the law has not been logic; it has been experience"—is true of history in general. Experience is a better predictor of future trends than is logic. And experience suggests that the unrealistic extremism that characterizes many young people often matures into more realistic centrism with age.

This is not to deny that one's commitment as a youth can have a significant impact on the ideologies, policies, and actions of later years. But aging often brings with it greater responsibility to others. And with that greater responsibility comes more nuance, increased willingness to compromise, and less commitment to ideological purity.

My thirty-year-old daughter reminds me that the liberalism of my youth—my anti-McCarthyism, my support for civil rights, my anti-war activism—was regarded as "extremist" or "radical" by some of my teachers, rabbis, and relatives. Although my values haven't changed much over the years, the goalposts demarcating the line between liberalism and radicalism have been moved over time. What was regarded as radical back in the day is viewed as merely liberal today. So it follows that when my daughter's generation takes over the world, what I regard as extremist today may become the new normal for centrism. To the extent that this new normal incorporates positive values—such as more widespread access to health care, higher education, immigration, and good jobs—that will be a welcome change. But to the extent that it incorporates the negative values of much of the radical hard-left—denial of free speech, due process, and tolerance for opposing views, as well as knee-jerk opposition to Israel—liberals must oppose them with the same fervor with which we have opposed hard-right illiberalism.

My daughter's point raises the broader question of whether there is really any objective standard by which to judge whether policies, attitudes, or actions are "extremist," or whether it is it generational and in the eye of the beholder. I think the answer may well be that it is generational as to some issues, such as universal single-payer healthcare, more open borders for immigration, and a wealth tax. But I certainly hope that all thinking people of every generation reject some signature issues of today's left-wing extremists, especially with regard to freedom of speech, due process, and identity politics. History has demonstrated that these are objectively extremist, and in my view objectively wrong positions, in *any* generation and regardless of the age of those espousing them. Moral relativism has its limits, and these extremist positions are wrong even by the most relativistic standards of morality, legality, and common sense.

Sacrificing free speech, due process, and other fundamental civil liberties is not only wrong, it is dangerous, because governmentally enforced certainty and uniformity of thought—which is the inevitable result of denial of civil liberties—denies us access to diversity of views and perspectives, which is essential to progress, the root of the word "progressive."

There are dangers, as well, in many of the extremist positions currently being espoused by young people on the hard-right, especially with regard to race, ethnicity, gender, and sexual orientation. There were many young people among those chanting racist slogans at

Charlottesville, and there are people of all ages espousing conspiracy theories regarding Covid-19. Some of the extremist—often bigoted—views expressed by young people on the right are the mirror images of views currently espoused by young extremists on the hard-left. Both groups believe that the world must be viewed through the lenses of race, ethnicity, gender, and sexual orientation. The hard-right sees these "identities" as negative, with their own identity being "superior." The hard-left sees these same identities as positive, with all others being unfairly "privileged." Both, I believe, are misguided, though the utterly negative bigotry of the hard-right is deserving of greater condemnation than the well-intentioned identity politics of the hard-left. But, as the great Justice Louis Brandeis cautioned: "The greatest dangers to liberty lurk in the insidious encroachment by men [and women] of zeal, well-meaning but without understanding."

Experience suggests that young extremists of the hard-right may be less likely than young extremists of the hard-left to moderate their bigoted views as they grow older. This may or may not be true of the current generation of extremists.[97]

So here is my prediction, based on my reading of history, my close connections with half a century of law school and college students, my observations of generational changes over my lifetime, and—despite my eschewal of wishful thinking—Martin Luther King's assessment that "The Arc of The Moral Universe . . . bends toward justice." I wish that were always the case. Slavery, the Holocaust, and other immoral epochs in our universe bent toward injustice. But, as my friend and teaching colleague, Steven Pinker, has demonstrated in his masterful book *The Better Angels of Our Nature*, the "secular trends" over many centuries would point to the world becoming a better place in terms of violence, warfare, and other threats to human life. Should that lead one to be an optimist when it comes to the dangers of extremism?

Jews traditionally answer questions with either other questions or with humorous stories. So I will respond by quoting a Jewish joke about the difference between a pessimist and an optimist: The pessimist says,

97 See Keinon, "Polling Shows Anti-Israel Positions of Youth Fade in U.S. with Age". *Jerusalem Post*, May 5, 2020

"Things are so bad they can't possibly get worse." The optimist responds: "Yes they can!"

So, with regard to the dangers of extremism, I believe that if nothing is done to combat the trends toward extremism, things can get worse. But I believe that "arcs" and "secular trends"—in whichever direction they are going—are subject to being influenced by ideas, experiences, policies, and actions. Those of us who believe that a dynamic centrist liberalism is better for our country and our world must make our case energetically and persuasively. The burden of proof is on us. The future of our world may be at stake. For a true liberal, inaction is not an option.

Alan Dershowitz is one of the most celebrated lawyers in the world. He was the youngest full professor in Harvard Law School history, where he is now the Felix Frankfurter Professor of Law, Emeritus. The author of numerous bestselling books, from *Chutzpah* to *Guilt by Accusation* to *The Case Against Impeaching Trump* to *The Best Defense* to *Reversal of Fortune* (which was made into an Academy Award–winning film) to *Defending Israel*, Dershowitz has advised presidents and prime ministers and has represented many prominent men and women, half of them pro bono.